PROMISES

THAT

PREVAIL

PROMISES

THAT

PREVAIL

LLOYD HILDEBRAND

Newberry, FL 32669

Bridge-Logos

Newberry, FL 32669

Promises That Prevail

By Lloyd Hildebrand

Printed in the United States of America.

Library of Congress Catalog Card Number: 2016937554

International Standard Book Number: 978-1-61036-157-6

Unless otherwise noted, all Scripture quotations are from the King James Version of the Holy Bible.

Scripture quotations marked NKJV are taken from the New King James Version of the Bible. Copyright 1979, 1980, 1982, by HarperCollins.

Dedication

This book is dedicated to you, a reader who loves God's Word. May you be richly blessed as you contemplate all God's promises to you. May you always prevail through the promises of God.

Contents

Introduction

Whereby are given unto us exceeding great and precious promises:
that by these ye might be partakers of the divine nature, having
escaped the corruption that is in the world through lust.

(2 PETER 1:4)

Our God is a great promise-keeper, and He wants you to be a promise-reaper. A promise-reaper is a person who believes God's promises, receives God's promises, stands upon God's promises, and walks upon God's promises. He accepts God's Word as living truth for his life. He knows that it is through the promises of God that he will prevail in all situations and circumstances.

The Bible abounds with God's personal promises to you. There are literally thousands of promises in God's Word. If you will learn to look upon these as His special promises to you, you will become a victorious believer. You will prevail.

Open the Bible to almost any random page, and you will discover a promise or several promises that you can take for your own life. Let me try this as I write. I've opened my Bible to the Book of Proverbs, chapter 28, verse 13: "He that covereth his sins shall not prosper: but whoso confesseth and forsaketh them shall have mercy." Now that's an important and wonderful promise, isn't it?

As we personalize the above verse, we realize that we must repent of our sins rather than trying to hide them. We must forsake ours sins and turn completely away from them. When we do so, we will receive God's mercy.

Try it for yourself, and see which one of God's promises is waiting for you to discover it. Searching for the promises is always an exciting adventure.

In this book you will learn about many of God's promises and how you can apply them to your life. This will result in so many blessings for you. Here are just a few of those promises:

- You are a new creation in Christ Jesus. (See 2 Corinthians 5:17.)
- You are the temple of the Holy Spirit. (See 1 Corinthians 6:9-17.)
- God gives you His benefits every day. (See Psalm 68:19.)
- God loves you with an everlasting love. (See Jeremiah 31:3.)
- All of your needs will be supplied. (See Philippians 4:19.)
- You are forgiven. (See Ephesians 4:32.)
- No weapon that is formed against you will prosper. (See Isaiah 54:17.)
- You have been adopted into the family of God. (See Romans 8:15.)
- The law of the Spirit of life (in Christ Jesus) has set you free from the law of sin and death. (See Romans 8:2.)

- The sufferings of this present time are not worthy to be compared with the glory that shall be revealed. (See Romans 8:18.)
- Nothing shall ever be able to separate you from the love of God. (See Romans 8:39.)
- The Lord takes pleasure in you. (See Psalm 147:11.)
- The joy of the Lord is your strength. (See Nehemiah 8:10.)

The above list gives you a good perspective on the wonderful promises of God, which are Yes and Amen in Christ Jesus. (See 1 Corinthians 1:20.)

As you read the Bible, look for any promises that are there for you to claim. Doing so makes Bible reading a very personal and exciting experience. I think you will be truly amazed by how many promises you will encounter almost every time you read the Word of God.

Be sure to meditate upon each one in such a way that you will fully realize what God is saying to you, and don't forget that the Bible is His book of promises to you. His promises are personal promises from Him to you.

Remember, these promises are for you and when you really believe them, your entire perspective on life will change. You will know beyond all doubt that God will keep His promises and fulfill His promises in your life. He is your faithful Father, and He loves to bless you.

"Now unto him that is able to do exceeding abundantly above all that we ask or think, according to the power that worketh in us, unto him be glory in the church by Christ Jesus throughout all ages, world without end. Amen" (Ephesians 3:20-21).

PART I

God's Great and Precious Promises

*Having therefore these promises, dearly
   beloved, let us*
*cleanse ourselves from all filthiness of the
   flesh and spirit,*
perfecting holiness in the fear of God.

(2 CORINTHIANS 7:1)

THE FIRST PROMISE I BELIEVED FROM THE BIBLE CAME TRUE

I was thirteen years old, and was attending a one-week summer camp at Camp Shadowbrook in the Pocono Mountains of Pennsylvania. It was such a wonderful place, and I had a great time there, meeting new friends and learning about things I had never heard before.

It was as if I had entered an entirely new world, an almost heavenly place. The people were so friendly, and the Bible was opened to me in a way that I had never experienced before. The camp had been founded by an evangelist named Percy Crawford, and his greatest desire was for everyone to know the Lord.

It was the best experience of my young life. One night after dark our counselor, who was called Mr. Dave, gathered us around a campfire, and he began to share God's Word with us. He told us about a promise from the Gospel of John that reached deep within my heart. When he read the words of this promise my heart began to pound. I truly believe it was Jesus knocking at the door of my heart: "He came unto his own, and his own received him not. But as many as received him, to them gave he power to become the sons of God, even to them that believe on his name" (John 1:12).

What powerful words, and what a wonderful promise. Mr. Dave went on to explain the verse to us, then he asked, "Would you like to receive Jesus as your Savior and Lord?"

Without hesitation, I said yes. As a result, I became a son of God, just as the verse had promised I would. Some might say that I couldn't have been that much of a sinner at age thirteen, and they would be somewhat right about that. However, a sinner I was, to be sure, because the Bible says, "For all have sinned, and come short of the glory of God" (Romans 3:23).

Yes, I knew I was a sinner, and I knew I needed a Savior. That August night I discovered that Jesus was my Savior. I received Him into my life, and I felt so clean and new. This was the first promise I had ever heard from the Bible, and it came true in my life. I knew I was a son of God, that my heavenly Father had adopted me into His family.

The folk at Camp Shadowbrook seemed to be such a real part of the family of God, and I will never forget them. Neither will I forget that night by the campfire, for it truly changed everything for me. As a result, I still know that Jesus lives within my heart, and His power is at work in my life.

Since then I've learned that all God's promises are true and I can depend on them. Many times I've stood upon His promises for healing, blessing, safety, provision, and other needs, and He has always come through for me and mine.

How I thank God for His faithfulness to His Word.

GOD ALWAYS DELIVERS ON HIS PROMISES

A promise is an agreement to do or not to do something. It is similar to a vow. A promise forms the basis for an expectation on the part of the one who has been promised something. A promise is a personal pledge from one person to another. Promises are meant to be kept, and God is always faithful to keep His promises. "It is of the Lord's mercies that we are not consumed, because his compassions fail not. They are new every morning: great is thy faithfulness" (Lamentations 3:22-23).

Charles H. Spurgeon loved to preach on the promises of God. He wrote, "The Bible is a book of precious promises! All the way we have to travel, they seem to be like a series of stepping stones across the stream of time, and we may march from one promise to another and never wet our feet all the way from Earth to Heaven if we do but know how to keep our eyes open and to find the right promise to step upon. 'All the promises'—the Old Testament ones as well as those in the New Testament—are sure and steadfast!"

I would like to offer my hearty amen to his comments about the promises. God will keep His promises— always, without fail, and completely. He is a very faithful Father to His children.

God's promises are like ripe fruit on a healthy tree. In order to get the fruit all we have to do is reach up and take it off the tree. It is then that we can enjoy its luscious flavor. The same is true with the promises of God. They are there for us to take freely and to enjoy their power through meditation. "Taste and see that the Lord is good. Blessed is the man that trusteth in him" (Psalm 34:8).

Standing on the promises leads us to trust God with every part of our lives, because through the promises He reveals His faithfulness and mercy to us.

This book includes many of the great and precious promises of God's Word, and I have written a brief meditation to go with each one. The meditations are designed to reveal God's loving heart to you, and to help you to grow in the grace and knowledge of the Lord. (See 2 Peter 3:18.)

Never forget that God has adopted you to be His child, and He has provided you with many promises on which to build your life. As your Father, He wants you to grow and to prosper. His promises hold the key to spiritual growth and blessedness. His promises help us to see Him as He really is.

Each of the promises of God in both the Old and New Testaments is very precious to me. Each one has substance that enables the believer to stand firm upon them and to walk according to them. It is as the old hymn by R. Kelso Carter says:

Standing on the promises of Christ my King,
Through eternal ages let His praises ring,
Glory in the highest I will shout and sing,
Standing on the promises of God.

(Refrain)

Standing on the promises that cannot fail,
When the howling storms of doubt and fear
*   assail,*
By the living Word of God I shall prevail,
Standing on the promises of God.

(Refrain)

Standing on the promises I now can see
Perfect, present cleansing in the blood for me;
Standing in the liberty where Christ makes
free,
Standing on the promises of God.

(Refrain)

Standing on the promises of Christ the Lord,
Bound to Him eternally by love's strong cord,
Overcoming daily with the Spirit's sword,
Standing on the promises of God.

(Refrain)

Standing on the promises I cannot fall,
Listening every moment to the Spirit's call
Resting in my Savior as my all in all,
Standing on the promises of God.

My friend, unless you are standing on the promises of God, you are standing on sinking sand. Jesus said, "Therefore whosoever heareth these sayings [including the promises] of mine, and doeth them, I will liken him unto a wise man, which built his house upon a rock: And the rain descended, and the floods came, and the winds blew, and beat upon that house; and it fell not: for it was founded upon a rock. And everyone that heareth these sayings of mine, and doeth them not, shall be likened unto a foolish man, which built his house upon the sand. And the rain descended, and the floods came, and the winds blew, and beat upon that house; and it fell: and great was the fall of it" (Matthew 7:24-27).

Jesus is the rock and He is the Word. (See John 1:1.) Therefore, to build our house upon the rock is to build it upon the promises of God. The hymnist says it well: "On Christ, the solid rock, I stand. All other ground is sinking sand." To avoid falling, therefore, we must take our stand on God's promises which cannot fail.

The promises of God, as Spurgeon said above, are stepping stones to progress in the Christian life. They are solid footholds for us to walk upon. W.A. Criswell wrote, "When our trials come, when we feel pain and suffering, when our tears flow again, it is our joy and comfort to lift our faces heavenward and to go on, standing on the promises of God."

PREVAILING FAITH

To prevail means to gain the advantage and to be victorious. To prevail is to triumph, to be successful, and to become stronger. The promises of God equip us to prevail in all the issues and challenges of life. Through the promises we become superior in spiritual strength, because we know God will always honor His Word.

Faith comes to you as you meditate upon God's words. Francis Chan, in his book entitled Overwhelmed by a Relentless God, writes, "True faith means holding nothing back. It means putting every hope in God's fidelity to His promises." This is the leap of faith, and underneath are the everlasting arms of our loving Father, which will catch us and lift us up.

11

Paul writes, "Faith cometh by hearing, and hearing by the word of God" (Romans 10:17). It is vitally important to realize that the key to faith is found in the Word of God, particularly in the promises of God.

This is why the writer to the Hebrews said, "Cast not away therefore your confidence, which hath great recompence of reward. For ye have need of patience, that, after ye have done the will of God, ye might receive the promise" (Hebrews 10:35-36). Confidence comes from faith, and faith requires patience. We must learn to wait in His presence for the answers to our prayers and the fulfillment of His promises.

Look at what happened to so many of the people of faith in the Old Testament. (See Hebrews 11.)

- By faith Abel offered a sacrifice that was acceptable to God.
- By faith Enoch was translated, and he never saw death.
- By faith Noah prepared an ark.
- By faith Abraham went out without knowing where he was going, but he received an overwhelming inheritance.
- By faith Sara received strength to conceive seed.
- By faith Isaac blessed Jacob and Esau concerning things to come.
- By faith Jacob blessed both the sons of Joseph.
- By faith Moses endured, as seeing Him who is invisible.
- By faith the Israelites passed through the Red Sea.
- By faith the walls of Jericho collapsed.

"And what shall I more say? For the time would fail me to tell of Gideon, and of Barak, and of Samson, and of Jephthae; of David, also, and Samuel, and of the prophets: Who through faith subdued kingdoms, wrought righteousness, obtained promises, stopped the mouths of lions, quenched the violence of fire, escaped the edge of the sword, out of weakness were made strong, waxed valiant in fight, turned to flight the armies of the aliens. Women received their dead raised to life again: and others were tortured, not accepting deliverance; that they might obtain a better resurrection: And others had trial of cruel mockings and scourgings, yea, moreover of bonds and imprisonment: They were stoned, they were sawn asunder. . . ." (Hebrews 11:32-37).

In the above examples we see the power of faith to enable God's people to prevail in all sorts of adverse circumstances. Prevailing faith is what is needed in order to act upon God's promises, and it is certainly what we need today. We must first believe and then we will receive what God has promised to us, so "Trust in the Lord with all thine heart; and lean not unto thine own understanding. In all thy ways acknowledge him, and he shall direct thy paths" (Proverbs 3:5-6).

Martin Luther wrote, "You are indicting your unbelief by distrusting God's goodness, and you are bringing greater misery upon yourself by dis-paraging God's blessing. For if you had trust in

God's grace and promises, you would undoubtedly be supported. But because you do not hope in the Lord, you will never prosper."

PART II

God's Word Cannot Fail

For the word of God is quick, and powerful, and sharper
than any twoedged sword, piercing even to the dividing
asunder of soul and spirit, and of the joints and marrow,
and is a discerner of the thoughts and intents of the heart.

(HEBREWS 4:12)

YOUR INHERITANCE

Imagine if someone had left you a large inheritance and said, "All you have to do is believe it and receive it." Surely you would want to obtain that inheritance as soon as possible.

God has done that for you through Jesus Christ. The Bible says, "Blessed be the God and Father of our Lord Jesus Christ, who hath blessed us with all spiritual blessings in heavenly places in Christ" (Ephesians 1:3, italics mine).

This is incredibly wonderful news, and it has already happened. All we have to do is believe it and receive it. The Sunday school chorus says, "Every promise in the Book is mine," and those promises involve all spiritual blessings.

These are already yours:

- Forgiveness
- Blessing
- Health and healing
- Salvation
- Victory
- Truth
- Guidance
- Love
- Power
- Hope
- Joy
- Peace
- Patience
- Self-control
- A sound mind
- All God's prevailing promises

All of these blessings are yours through faith, and there are many more as well. This book reveals what your inheritance in Christ Jesus is, as it shares His wonderful promises with you.

PSALM 119

Psalm 119 is filled with God's promises. It shares what God can do for us through His Word, and His Word is a major part of your spiritual inheritance. Let's review some of those promises here:

Verses 1-2: You are blessed as you walk in His ways and keep His testimonies.

Verse 6: You will not be ashamed as you walk according to His Word.

Verse 8: God will not forsake you.

Verse 9: You are cleansed as you take heed to His Word.

Verse 11: The Word of God will keep you from sin.

Verse 17: God will deal bountifully with you.

Verse 18: Your spiritual eyes will be opened.

Verse 24: God's testimonies are your delight and your counselors.

Verse 25: God's Word gives life to you.

Verse 28: God's Word strengthens you.

Verse 41: God's mercies come to you as you meditate upon His Word.

Verse 42: Trusting in God's Word enables you to give answers to others.

Verse 45: You will walk at liberty.

Verse 50: God's Word is your comfort in times of affliction.

Verse 57: God is your portion.

Verse 66: God's Word teaches you good judgment and knowledge.

Verse 77: God's tender mercies will come to you.

Verse 80: Your heart will be sound.

Verse 98: God's Word gives you wisdom.

Verse 99: God's Word gives you spiritual understanding.

Verse 105: God's Word is a lamp unto your feet and a light unto your path.

Verse 111: God's Word is your heritage forever.

Verse 114: God's Word gives you hope.

Verse 117: God's Word holds you up and keeps you safe.

Verse 130: The entrance of God's words gives you light.

Verse 144: Through God's Word you are made righteous.

Verse 153: Deliverance comes through God's Word.

The above list shows just a few of God's promises that are found in Psalm 119, but this partial list reveals how powerful the Word of God is and what a treasure chest it is. Your spiritual inheritance in Christ is far better than anything this world has to offer.

The Psalmist writes, "I rejoice at thy word, as one that findeth great spoil" (Psalm 119: 162). The promises of God give us a great cause for rejoicing.

Corrie ten Boom wrote, "Gather the riches of God's promises. Nobody can take away for you those texts from the Bible which you have learned by heart." She also said, "Let God's promises shine on your problems."

THE PERMANENCE OF GOD'S CHARACTER

A.W. Pink wrote, "The permanence of God's character guarantees the fulfillment of His promises." This is so very true, because we know God cannot lie. He is always faithful to fulfill His promises; He will never go back on His Word.

God is. . .

- Love
- Faithful
- All-powerful
- All-knowing
- Always there
- Truth
- Perfect
- Righteous
- Good
- Merciful
- Compassionate
- Your Father
- Your Counselor
- Wise
- Eternal
- Unlimited

- Your strength
- The great I Am
- The beginning and the end
- The Alpha and Omega
- Your Shepherd
- Your Deliverer
- Your Redeemer
- Almighty
- Incapable of sinning
- Your healer
- Your hope
- Your guide

We could continue with this list of the attributes of God, for there are so many. The important thing to know is that God cannot fail. He is ". . . able to do exceeding abundantly above all that we ask or think, according to the power that worketh in us" (Ephesians 3:20).

He is the great Promise-keeper, as we see in the following examples:

- God promised Abraham that in his seed all nations would be blessed. Through the Hebrew nation a Savior came and through Him mighty blessings have come to the whole world, to all those who believe on the name of Jesus.
- God promised the Hebrews that they would prosper as a nation if they faithfully served Him. It was through the Hebrew nation that the concept of monotheism (belief in one God) developed.
- God promises David that his family would reign over God's people forever. This was fulfilled

in Jesus, the Messiah—the great King of the endless kingdom. He reigns now, and He will reign forever.

These are more than promises; they are covenants that God has made with people. A covenant is a binding and solemn agreement made by two or more individuals. It is a compact, solid, and inviolable agreement.

God wants to be in a covenant relationship with us. He wants to have intimacy and fellowship with us. His Word states, "That which we have seen and heard declare we unto you, that ye also may have fellowship with us: and truly our fellowship is with the Father, and with his Son Jesus Christ. And these things write we unto you, that your joy may be full" (1 John 1:3-4).

Intimacy with God that comes from a covenantal relationship always results in joy for the believer. How could it be otherwise? God is your Abba-Father, your Creator, the One who loves you with an everlasting love.

He is faithful and true, and He wants you to learn to trust Him fully. "His compassions fail not. They are new every morning. Great is thy faithfulness. The Lord is my portion, saith my soul: therefore will I hope in him" (Lamentations 3:22-24).

It is impossible for God to lie to you. When He promises something to you, He will do it. D.L. Moody wrote, "God never made a promise that was too good to be true."

Never believe the devil's lie that things will never change. Put your hope in God and His Word. His special promises are for you. Believe them, receive them, and take your stand upon them.

PART III

All God's Promises Are Yes and Amen

For all the promises of God in Him are Yes,
and in Him Amen, to the
glory of God through us.

(2 CORINTHIANS 1:20)

AFFIRM THE PROMISES WITH YOUR WORDS AND ACTIONS

The promises of God help us to keep a positive perspective on our life and circumstances. They are always Yes and Amen. Speak them forth, and don't let negative words spoil your ability to receive them.

Life and death are in the power of your tongue. (See Proverbs 18:21.) If you speak the promises of God on a daily basis, you will be filled with faith, and this faith is what will enable you to appropriate them for your life. They will bring life and vitality to you and cause all negativity to cease.

As often as possible, speak them aloud, so that you will hear their important words. This makes a tremendous difference. It is a form of praise, and we know that God inhabits the praises of His people. The promises are very helpful, also, in helping you wage spiritual warfare. One of the weapons of your warfare is the word of your testimony, and, as you incorporate the promises of God with the word of your testimony, God moves in supernatural ways.

"And they overcame him [the devil] by the blood of the Lamb, and by the word of their testimony; and they loved not their lives unto the death" (Revelation 12:11).

The promises of God enable you to become an overcomer in spiritual warfare. That's why I call them *Promises That Prevail*. Through God's promises you will prevail over all forces that may come against you. The Bible says, "Ye are of God, little children, and have overcome them: because greater is he that is in you, than he that is in the world" (1 John 4:4).

This is a prevailing promise that stands the test of truth. Stand upon it, speak it forth, and you will be a victor in the circumstances of your life.

THE TONGUE OF THE WISE IS HEALTH

Speaking the promises brings health to your body, soul, and spirit. As you speak God's promises, you learn to stop uttering negative words and phrases. This pleases God, and it helps you to be happy.

"And my tongue shall speak of thy righteousness and of thy praise all the day long" (Psalm 35:28). Let the promises of God guide you in what you say and how you say it.

"My tongue also shall talk of thy righteousness all the day long" (Psalm 71:24).

Both of these verses use the phrase "all the day long," and I think this is very important. We don't just speak of God's righteousness and His promises from time to time, but we should be speaking them forth all day long. All day long!

God's promises have been given to us according to the purpose of His will. Like God, they are unfailing and unchangeable. As God fulfills His promises, He receives glory and we receive blessing upon blessing. Hallelujah!

God's truth is entwined with His promises. His truth is inviolable, inerrant, and immutable. I hear some people saying, "This will happen if it is God's will." However, we already know what God's will is with regard to most of the circumstances of life. His promises reveal His will to us, so it is possible to know what His will is in any given situation.

God's character is entwined with His promises. God will not let you down. What He says, He will do. He simply cannot do otherwise, because He is righteous, honorable, and completely trustworthy.

God's power is entwined with His promises. What He promises to you, He will always be able to perform.

God's love is entwined with His promises. It is because He loves you that He has given you these wonderful promises. Remember, He loves you with an everlasting love. Here is God's promise to you: "Ask, and it shall be given you; seek, and ye shall find; knock, and it shall be opened unto you: for every one that asketh receiveth; and he that seeketh findeth; and to him that knocketh it shall be opened. Or what man is there of you, whom if his son ask bread, will give him a stone? Or if he ask a fish, will give him a serpent? If ye then, being evil, know how to give good gifts unto your children, how much more shall your Father which is in heaven give good things to them that ask him?" (Matthew 7:7-11).

God knows what you have need of, and He promises to supply your need according to His riches in glory by Christ Jesus. (See Philippians 4:19.)

Proclaim these truths with your tongue, and remember these words: "The tongue of the wise useth knowledge aright" (Proverbs 15:2).

Let's review some of the Scriptures that relate to the use of our tongues:

"A wholesome tongue is a tree of life"

(PROVERBS 15:4)

"Whoso keepeth his mouth and his tongue keepeth his soul from troubles

(PROVERBS 21:23)

"Keep thy tongue from evil, and thy lips from speaking guile"

(PSALM 34:13)

As you can see, the way we use our tongues is vitally important. We must speak words of life, not death; of hope, not despair; of trust, not doubt; of victory, not defeat; of truth, not falsehood; of positive thoughts, not negativity; and of abundance, not lack.

Positive words breed positive thoughts, and positive thoughts breed positive actions. Stay positive at all times. This is being proactive in promise-centered living. Keep your focus on the promises of God instead of the problems of life.

ALL GOD'S PROMISES

All God's promises are for you. You can reach out and receive them by faith. Someone said there are more than 7000 promises in the Word of God, and each one is for you.

God promises so much to you (and, remember, many of these blessings have already been given to you):

- Abundance
- Redemption
- Justification
- Forgiveness
- Pardon
- The Holy Spirit
- Supply

- Providence
- Healing
- Truth
- Sanctification
- Guidance
- Resurrection
- Wisdom
- Safety
- Peace
- Joy
- Patience
- Glory
- Eternal life
- Comfort
- Mercy

And these are just some of the promises God has given to you. Do you see that many of these have already been given to you? You don't need to ask for wisdom, for example, because it is already yours. Righteousness is yours, as well, because of this promise: 'For he hath made him to be sin for us, who knew no sin: that we might be made the righteousness of God in him" (2 Corinthians 5:21).

God's Word is a cornucopia of blessings for us. Every day in every way His promises shine brighter and brighter, and they provide so much for us. His promises are so secure and certain that you can literally build your life upon them.

The multitude of God's promises are Yes and Amen in Christ Jesus. Martin Luther wrote, "You are indicting your unbelief by distrusting God's goodness, and you are bringing greater misery upon yourself by disparaging God's blessing. For if you had trust in God's grace and promises, you would undoubtedly be supported. But because you do not hope in the Lord, you will never prosper."

Trusting in all God's promises is a lifeline that will keep you from sinking. They are a sure foundation that will never crumble. You can count on everything God promises to you.

Read His Word. Meditate upon His promises. Receive everything that God wants to give to you. All you have to do is believe what He tells you, for it is in believing that you receive.

GOD WILL NOT CHANGE HIS MIND

"God is not a man, that he should lie; neither the son of man, that he should repent: hath he said, and shall he not do it? or hath he spoken, and shall he not make it good?" (Numbers 23:19). We could ask a few other rhetorical questions: Does God speak and not act? Does God promise and not fulfill? Does God hold out false hope to us? Can God fail? Is there anything God cannot do?

We know the answers to these questions:

- God does not lie.
- God does not mislead.
- God does not deceive.
- God does not change His mind.

29

- God does not hold out false hope.
- God does not tempt us.
- God does not repent.

God's character leads Him to:

- Keep all His promises.
- Be totally reliable.
- Love us as His children.
- Bless us.
- Fulfill His Word to us.

Joshua said, "And ye know in all your hearts and in all your souls, that not one thing hath failed of all the good things which the Lord your God spake concerning you; all are come to pass unto you, and not one thing hath failed thereof" (Joshua 23:14).

Promise-centered living is a life style that opens the door to God's best in your life. Let His promises lead you to great things in Him!

PART IV

Personal Promises From God to You

By which have been given to us exceedingly great and precious promises,
that through these you may be partakers of the divine nature, having escaped the corruption
that is In the world through lust.

(2 PETER 1:4)

The promises of God come to us from a vast treasury in Heaven. They are personal promises from the Father to you. All you have to do is believe them, receive them, and let them bring faith to your heart. These "great and precious promises" will enable you to take part in the divine nature and to escape the corruption that is in the world as a result of evil desires.

Let's take a look at some of those promises:

1. You are saved. (See John 6:47).
2. God loves you forever. (See Jeremiah 31:3.)

3. Your body is the temple of the Holy Spirit. (See 1 Corinthians 6:19-20).

4. God has chosen you as His own. (See John 15:16).

5. Christ lives within you. (See Colossians 1:27).

6. The indwelling Christ is your hope of glory. (See Colossians 1:27.)

7. The Father will supply all your needs. (See Philippians 4:19.)

8. God promises to restore health to you. (See Jeremiah 30:17.)

9. God forgives you when you confess your sins to Him. (See 1 John 1:9.)

10. It is impossible for anything to separate you from the love of God. (See Romans 8:38-39.)

11. You are never alone. (See Hebrews 13:5.)

12. The Lord is your Shepherd. (See Psalm 23:1.)

13. Heaven is your home. (See Psalm 23:6.)

14. You will flourish. (See Psalm 92:12.)

15. God has overcome the world and so can you. (See 1 John 5:4.)

16. You can expect to receive when you pray. (See Mark 11:24.)

17. God cares deeply about you. (See 1 Peter 5:7.)

18. Your faith is growing. (See Romans 10:17.)

19. Your patience will be rewarded. (See Hebrews 6:12.)

20. Angels are watching over you. (See Psalm 91:11-12.)

21. God's Word will guide you. (See Psalm 119:105.)

22. All things are possible to you. (See Mark 9:23.)
23. God will renew your strength.
    (See Isaiah 40:31.)
24. All things will work together for good in your
    life. (See Romans 8:28.)
25. No evil will befall you. (See Psalm 91:10.)
26. You are justified. (See Romans 3:24.)
27. God loads you with benefits.
    (See Psalm 68:19.)
28. You are a new creation in Christ.
    (See 2 Corinthians 5:17.)
29. Perfect peace is yours. (See Isaiah 26:3.)
30. God gives you His rest. (See Hebrews 4:1.)
31. You are a child of God. (See Romans 8:16.)
32. God will keep you safe. (See Proverbs 18:10.)
33. God has adopted you into His family.
    (Romans 8:15.)
34. There is now no condemnation for you.
    (See Romans 8:1.)
35. The law of the Spirit of life in Christ Jesus has
    set you free from the law of sin and death.
    (See Romans 8:2.)
36. The Spirit of God is giving life to your mortal
    body. (See Romans 8:11.)
37. Healing will come. (See Psalm 107:20.)
38. You can move mountains. (See Mark 11:23.)
39. The joy of the Lord is your strength.
    (See Nehemiah 8:10.)
40. God's way is perfect, and He is a buckler to
    you as you trust in Him. (See Psalm 18:30.)
41. God hears your prayer. (See 1 John 5:14.)

42. God's Word will keep you from sin.
    (See Psalm 119:11.)
43. God will reward your faith.
    (See Hebrews 11:6.)
44. The Lord takes pleasure in you.
    (See Psalm 147:11.)
45. God wants you to prosper. (See 3 John 2.)
46. God is at work in your life, and His work in your
    life will continue. (See Philippians 1:6.)
47. You will never be ashamed.
    (See 2 Timothy 2:15.)
48. God will fulfill His promises in your life.
    (See Hebrews 10:23.)
49. God will order your steps. (See Psalm 37:23.)
50. There is a crown of life reserved for you.
    (See James 1:12.)
51. You can experience everlasting joy.
    (See Isaiah 51:12.)
52. Nothing shall be able to offend you.
    (See Psalm 119:165.)
53. No weapon that is formed against you shall
    prosper. (See Isaiah 54:17.)
54. You can do all things through Christ because
    He strengthens you. (See Philippians 4:13.)
55. You are blessed with all spiritual blessings
    in heavenly places in Christ.
    (See Ephesians 1: 3.)
56. God is able to do exceedingly abundantly
    beyond all that you could ask or think.
    (See Ephesians 3:20.)
57. You will be fruitful in every good work.
    (See Colossians 1:10.)

58. You are increasing in the knowledge of God. (See Colossians 1:10.)
59. You are being strengthened with all might. (See Colossians 1:11.)
60. The peace of God is ruling in your heart. (See Colossians 3:15.)

I have turned each of the above sixty promises into a positive affirmation of faith on which you can take your stand. You can do the same with more than 6,000 other promises that are found throughout God's Word.

The key to receiving these promises is believing them. Let faith arise in your heart. Reach out and take these promises into your own life. Stand upon them. God loves you, and He is faithful to every promise in His Word.

Are you excited as you meditate upon God's promises? They form a vital connection between your heart and God's. You can stand upon, walk upon, and run with the promises of God. God's special promises to you enable you to:

- *Walk in newness of life.*
- *Walk in confidence.*
- *Walk in faith.*
- *Walk in trust.*
- *Walk according to the Spirit.*
- *Walk circumspectly.*
- *Walk honestly.*
- *Walk in good works.*
- *Walk worthy of God's calling in your life.*

- *Walk in Christ.*
- *Walk differently from other Gentiles.*
- *Walk in love.*
- *Walk in grace.*
- *Walk as a child of the light.*
- *Walk in wisdom.*
- *Walk in truth.*
- *Walk according to His commandments.*
- *Walk in the fear of the Lord.*
- *Walk with a sense of purpose.*
- *Walk without falling.*
- *Walk in hope.*
- *Walk in faithfulness.*
- *Walk in integrity.*
- *Walk with God.*
- *Walk in victory.*

My friend, walking according to the above list is walking according to God's Word and all His promises. In the pages that follow (in Part VI), you will find many Bible promises arranged under specific topics. Please meditate on these for your spiritual grown and edification.

I know you will be thrilled by the sheer magnitude of God's grace as it is revealed in each of these promises, which I've personalized for you so that you can readily apply them to your own heart and life. I pray that you will personally experience the power of each of these promises as you reflect upon their truth.

PART V

The Promises of God in the Names of God

The names of God are worthy of our contemplation, because they reveal so many of God's promises to us. Each of His names is a source of power that propels us to prevail through His promises and His purposes for us. In this chapter we will look briefly at some of the names of God from the Old Testament, the various names of Jesus, and the names of the Holy Spirit.

OLD TESTAMENT NAMES OF GOD

Adonai. He is the great God of the universe, and He is our Master and Lord. Adonai is the name of God that reveals His sovereign and total authority over all.

Elohim. He is the omnipotent, omnipresent, and omniscient Creator of the universe. He knows everything and He is present everywhere. He is the God who is there at all times.

El Roi. He is the God who sees us and everything about us, including all the circumstances of our lives. He knows all about us, and He cares.

El Shaddai. He is the all-suffcent One. He is Almighty God—the all-powerful One. He is the source of all our blessings, and there is no problem too big for Him to handle perfectly. He does all things well.

Immanuel. The God who is always with us. He is the great I Am. Our God never changes. His promises never fail. He is always faithful to us, and He wants us to obey Him.

Jehovah. God is the self-existent One. He is worthy of all our worship, honor, devotion, and respect.

Jehovah-Rapha. He is the Lord who heals. In the Lord we find the ultimate cure for all kinds of sicknesses and afflictions—physical, emotional, mental, and spiritual. He truly is the Great Physician.

Jehovah-Rohi. He is the Lord, our Shepherd. He protects, supplies our needs, guards us, watches over us, knows us, and leads us. He is both tender and strong. He knows us and loves us with an everlasting love.

Jehovah-Tsidkenu. God is our righteousness. He imparts His righteousness to us. Jesus became sin for us so that we would become His righteousness.

YHWH—This is another rendering of the name *Jehovah*—the I Am, the self-existent One. Even when we are faithless, He is faithful.

THE NAMES OF JESUS

Emmanuel/Immanuel. God is with us. He is the only begotten Son of God. He became one of us so that we could be with Him forever.

The King of kings. Jesus is our sovereign Lord. He is the King of kings and Lord of lords. He is our Master and the Prince of peace. He is the King over all rulers, and we are the subjects of His kingdom.

The Lord of lords. He rules over all His creation and His church.

Messiah. Jesus is the Anointed One. The Hebrew word messiah is translated into Greek as Christ.

The Wonderful Counselor. Jesus is our advocate, redeemer, comforter, and judge. As our counselor, He comforts and consoles us with compassion and understanding. He defends us like a lawyer, and He offered himself as payment for our sins.

Almighty. Jesus is all-powerful. All power in Heaven and in Earth resides in Him, and He resides in you. He is mighty as He battles in our behalf. Nothing is impossible for Him.

Everlasting Father. Jesus was involved in the creation of all things. Like God the Father, He has no beginning or ending. He is the everlasting One, and, as such, He is the source of time, space, and all creation.

The Prince of Peace. Jesus is our peace. We can know no peace without knowing Him. By His death

39

on the cross He put an end to the conflict between God and mankind.

Redeemer. He is our Redeemer. By dying on the cross, Christ redeemed us from sin, Satan, the powers of darkness, and the debt we owe to God's law.

The Son of God. Jesus is the only begotten Son of God. He partakes fully in the divine life. Through Christ, we become children of God by adoption.

THE NAMES OF THE HOLY SPIRIT

The Breath of Almighty God. He is the life-giving Spirit that connects us to God and breathes His life and power into us. He is divine inspiration.

Counselor/Comforter. The Holy Spirit counsels us, comforts us, teaches us, and gives us strength and power. When we are troubled He intercedes for us. He is the divine Paraclete.

Spirit of Counsel. The Holy Spirit guides us and teaches us. He leads us into all truth.

The Eternal Spirit. He is the everlasting Spirit of God. He loves us eternally.

The Free Spirit. The Holy Spirit is free and generous. He is always willing to bless us. It is in and through Him that we find spiritual freedom.

God. The Holy Spirit is God, the third Person of the Holy Trinity. He is not just a force; He is a person. He is one person in the triune Godhead.

Good Spirit. The Holy Spirit is good. He will lead us and teach us about all that is truly good. The Holy Spirit is always with us to guide us and keep us.

The Holy Spirit. Yes, He is holy, and He is the Spirit of holiness. He is God present with us.

The Power of the Highest. He is the greatest power that has ever existed. He enables us to accomplish so many things that we would be unable to do without Him. He is all-powerful.

The above discussion of God's names reveals some of His promises to us. They are promises of love, protection, power, security, comfort, purpose, and strength. Through the names of God we truly find many *Promises That Prevail.*

PART VI

Promises That Prevail

The topics within this section are applicable to our lives. They are listed alphabetically for easy reference. These devotionals are ideal for quiet time, personal study, group study, and biblical meditation. My prayer is that you will be greatly blessed as you read these promise-based meditations.

1

Abiding in Christ

Affirmation of Faith: I will abide in Christ, and I know He will abide in me. This is the key to fruitfulness in my life.

> *I am the vine, ye are the branches: he that*
> *   abideth in me,*
> *and I in him, the same bringeth forth much*
> *   fruit: for without me*
> *ye can do nothing.*

(JOHN 15:5)

Central Focus: To abide in Christ is to remain in Him, to make Him your abode and your dwelling place. The person who does this will be fruitful. Here is a prayer promise from Him: "If ye abide in me, and my words abide in you, ye shall ask what ye will, and it shall be done unto you" (John 15:7). It is clear that God will answer your prayers if you abide in Christ.

Meditation on God's Promises to You: The Lord Jesus Christ is my abiding place. Without Him I can do nothing, but through Him I can do all things, for

He strengthens me. As I abide in the Lord and ask what I will, I know He will answer my prayers.

Abiding in the Lord gives me great confidence. I know that when He shall appear, I will not be ashamed before Him at His coming. Through God's grace I am able to keep His Word, and His love is perfected in me. I will abide in Him and walk as He walked.

It is in Him that I live and move and have my being. I will abide in the doctrine of Christ. How I thank God that I have both the Father and the Son in my life.

The Lord's anointing abides in me and it teaches me all things. Therefore, I have no need for others to teach me, because His anointing teaches me all things. It is truth, and it leads me to abide in Christ.

I will dwell in the secret place of the Most High, and I will abide under the shadow of the Almighty. The Word of God has brought cleansing to me, and it has renewed my mind as I abide in the Lord. Because the Lord has grafted me into the vine of life, I am able to bear much fruit. Praise His holy name!

The Father prunes and trims me so that I will become ever more fruitful. As a result, the Father will be glorified, I will be full of fruit, and my fruitfulness will show others that I am a disciple of Jesus Christ. I will ever abide in Jesus' great love for me.

It will always be my desire to follow in the footsteps of my Master. I am in Him, and He is within me. Jesus prayed that I would be one with my brothers and sisters in Him. He said that as He and the Father are one, so would believers be with each other. I want to learn how to be one with Him and with my brothers and sisters, so that the world will believe that Jesus is the Christ.

Abiding in Christ is my safe place. He is my refuge and my hiding place. He is my security and my strength. I will abide in Him forever.

Related Scriptures: John 15:4; John 15:5; Philippians 4:13; John 15:7; 1 John 2:28; 1 John 2:5-6; Acts 17:28; 2 John 1:9; 1 John 2:27; Psalm 91:1; John 15:3; Romans 12:2; John 15:5; John 15:2; John 15:8; John 15:10; 1 Peter 2:21; Acts 17:28; 1 John 3:24; John 17:21.

Personal Prayer: Father, I thank you for the life that flows through the True Vine which is Jesus Christ. It thrills me to know that you have given Him all authority in Heaven and in Earth, and He (the all-powerful One) now lives in me. As I learn to abide more and more in Jesus, I know my fruitfulness will abound. It is always my desire to glorify you, Father, and I thank you so much for allowing me to be in Christ and for Him to be in me. In Jesus' name, Amen.

A Promise to Claim: "If ye abide in me, and my words abide in you, ye shall ask what ye will, and it will be done unto you" (John 15:7).

Words of Wisdom: *"God is most glorified in us when we are most satisfied in Him"* (John Piper).

2

Abundance

Affirmation of Faith: I am abounding in all God's blessings. Spiritual abundance is mine.

> *I am come that they might have life, and that they*
> *might have it more abundantly.*

(JOHN 10:10)

Central Focus: Jesus wants you to experience all the fullness of His abundant life. Abundant living means that your life is full of blessing, honor, glory, provision, and joy, and it cannot compare with anything this world offers. He gives from His abundance so that we will be able to live abundantly in this world.

Meditation on God's Promises to You: Spiritual abundance is mine through Christ Jesus. My Father loves to give good things to me. He is the Father of lights with whom there is no variableness nor shadow of turning. He is the Giver of every good and perfect gift.

I will let the Word of Christ dwell in me richly in all wisdom. I will delight myself in God's statutes and I will not forget His Word. God has always dealt well with me according to His Word. Not one word of all His good promises has ever failed. I will sing of His mercies forever.

My Father wants me to experience His abundance, fullness, and wholeness in every area of my life. I receive His abundance now. I believe that my God wants me to prosper and be in good health. He blesses me with an abundance of provision.

The Lord supplies all my needs according to His riches in glory by Christ Jesus. I will never want for anything. He has brought me into a place of abundance. Praise His holy name. God, my heavenly Father, always gives me the desires of my heart.

I give Him first place in my life, as I seek His kingdom and His righteousness, and, as I do so, I know He will bless me and add all things unto me. I cast all my cares upon Him, for I know He cares for me. Godliness with contentment is great gain for me.

Jesus is everything to me. He's all I need. He is my Savior and my Lord. Hallelujah for the abundance I find in Him.

Related Scriptures: James 1:17; Colossians 3:16; Psalm 119:16; Psalm 119:65; 1 Kings 8:56; Psalm 89:1; John 1:16; Mark 5:34; 3 John 2; Nehemiah 2:20; Philippians 4:19; Psalm 23:1; 2 Corinthians 9:11; Psalm 37:4; Matthew 6:33; 1 Peter 5:7; 1 Timothy 6:6.

Personal Prayer: Dear Lord, you are my Shepherd. You have given so much to me. I love you for all the protection, care, and supply you have provided for me. I know I shall never have to want for anything, for you always supply all my need according to your riches in glory by Christ Jesus. Thank you for all the unsearchable riches you've given for me to enjoy. Thank you for always meeting all my needs. I am so blessed to be your child. In Jesus' name I pray, Amen.

A Promise to Claim: "I am come that they might have life, and that they might have it more abundantly" (John 10:10).

Words of Wisdom: *"We are to be shut out from men, and shut in with God"* (Andrew Murray).

3

Anger

Affirmation of Faith: I know that human wrath does not work the righteousness of God, so I will avoid it at all times. Anger is a destructive force, so I will learn to deal with it in positive ways.

> *A wrathful man stirreth up strife: but he that is slow*
> *to anger appeaseth strife.*

(PROVERBS 15:18)

Central Focus: Anger (unless it truly is righteous indignation) is devoid of the righteousness of God. (See James 1:19-20.) It is possible to overcome a tendency to anger by standing on God's promises. His promises prevail over anger, as God, by His Spirit, enables you to be an overcomer. You can do all things through Christ who strengthens you. (See Philippians 4:13.)

Meditation on God's Promises to You: People who are slow to wrath have great spiritual understanding. Such a person is unusual, but I will become such a person through the grace of Christ. He teaches me that a soft answer turns anger away, but a harsh word stirs anger up.

With God's help I will remove all bitterness, wrath, anger, and clamor from my life. I will put away all malice and evil speaking. Instead, I will be kind to others, tender-hearted, and forgiving, even as God for Christ's sake has forgiven me.

I will never let the sun go down upon my feelings of anger. God has not appointed me to wrath, but to obtain salvation through the Lord Jesus Christ. God is helping me to put off all these: anger, wrath, malice, blasphemy, and filthy language.

From now on I will be swift to hear, slow to speak, and slow to get angry, because I know this is what God wants from me. I realize that anger rests in the bosom of fools. A quick-tempered person acts foolishly.

I know that vengeance belongs to God, not to me. Therefore, I surrender my "right" to self-defense and anger. Walking with Jesus, I will give food to my enemy when he is hungry and water to him when he is thirsty. In so doing, I will heap coals of fire on his head and the Lord will reward me. Hallelujah!

God tells me that one who is slow to anger is better than the mighty, and he who rules his spirit is better than he who takes a city. With God's help I will always be slow to anger and I will learn to rule my spirit. I will bear the fruit of the Spirit in all the relationships and responsibilities of my life, and this includes self-control.

The Holy Spirit will control me in place of anger and I will walk in Him so I will not fulfill the lusts of my flesh.

Related Scriptures: Proverbs 14:29; Proverbs 15:1; Ephesians 4:31-32; Ephesians 4:26; 1 Thessalonians 5:9; Colossians 3:8; James 1:19; Ecclesiastes 7:9; Proverbs 14:17; Hebrews 10:30; Proverbs 25:21-22; Proverbs 16:32; Galatians 5:22-23.

Personal Prayer: Abba-Father, I will be your son indeed. I realize that this means that I should not let anger overtake me. Help me always to replace any impulse to anger with a heart of understanding and forgiveness. Thank you for showing me how to overcome wrath through a soft answer. It is my desire to always deal with others with grace and gentleness. In Jesus' name, Amen.

A Promise to Claim: "For God hath not appointed us to wrath, but to obtain salvation by our Lord Jesus Christ" (1 Thessalonians 5:9).

Words of Wisdom: *"Thou hast created us for thyself, and our heart is restless until it finds its rest in thee"* (St. Augustine).

4

Anxiety

Affirmation of Faith: Anxiety is a form of fear, and God's perfect love in my life leaves no room for fear.

> *Be careful for nothing; but in every thing by prayer and supplication*
> *with thanksgiving let your requests be made known unto God. And*
> *the peace of God, which passeth all understanding, shall keep your hearts and minds through Christ Jesus.*

(PHILIPPIANS 4:6-7)

Central Focus: You are free from fear, free from guilt, free from condemnation, and free from all anxiety when you place your full trust in the Lord. Anxiety vanishes in His restful presence.

Meditation on God's Promises to You: My heart is not troubled because I believe in God and in His Son, Jesus Christ. His peace has been imparted to me and this keeps my heart from being troubled or anxious. The Father keeps me in perfect peace as I stay my mind on Him. I trust Him with everything in my life.

Having been justified by faith, I have peace with God through my Lord Jesus Christ. I choose to be spiritually minded, not carnally minded, because I know this will bring life and peace to me. I realize that the Kingdom of God does not consist of eating and drinking, but of righteousness, peace, and joy in the Holy Spirit.

Great peace is mine because I love God and His Word. The God of love and peace is always with me. Hallelujah! I cast all my cares upon the Lord, for I know He cares for me. Jesus wants me to come unto Him, and I do so now. He gives me His peace and rest. I take His yoke upon myself and I choose to learn of Him, for His yoke is easy and His burden is light.

As I seek first the Lord's kingdom and His righteousness, He adds all other things to me. He is supplying all my needs according to His riches in glory by Christ Jesus. I will trust in the Lord with all my heart and I will not lean upon my own understanding. As a result, I know He will direct all my steps.

I praise God that He has freed me from all anxiety.

Related Scriptures: John 14:1; John 14:27; Isaiah 26:3; Romans 5:1; Romans 8:6; Romans 14:17-19; Psalm 119:165; 2 Corinthians 13:11; 1 Peter 5:7; Matthew 11:28-30; Matthew 6:33; Philippians 4:19; Proverbs 3:5-6.

Personal Prayer: Heavenly Father, thank you for showing me how to rise above any anxiety or worry in my life. Through your grace I will be completely free of all anxiety. Thank you for keeping me in perfect peace as I keep my mind stayed on you. Your peace and rest enable me to face all circumstances with confidence and strength. Your peace surpasses all understanding and I know it will guard my heart and my mind through Christ Jesus. In His name I pray, Amen.

A Promise to Claim: "Be careful [anxious] for nothing; but in everything by prayer and supplication with thanksgiving let your requests be made known to God. And the peace of God, which passeth all understanding, shall keep your hearts and minds through Christ Jesus" (Philippians 4:6-7).

Words of Wisdom: *"In comparison with this big world, the human heart is only a small thing. Though the world is so large, it is utterly unable to satisfy this tiny heart. The ever-growing soul and its capacity can be satisfied only in the infinite God. As water is restless until it reaches its level, so the soul has no peace until it rests in God"* (Sadhu Sundar Singh).

5

Blessings

Affirmation of Faith: I will never forget that God's blessings flood my life with joy on a daily basis.

*Blessed be the God and Father of our Lord
Jesus Christ, who
hath blessed us with all spiritual blessings
in heavenly places in Christ.*

(EPHESIANS 1:3)

Central Focus: The blessings of God are falling upon you, following you, and filling you. You are blessed beyond all measure. Count your blessings. Realize all that God has done for you.

Meditation on God's Promises to You: I am already blessed with all spiritual blessings in heavenly places in Christ. His blessing in my life helps me to prosper in every way, and He adds no sorrow to it. As I learn to listen to Him and obey Him, His blessings overtake me. He blesses me in every place and in every way. Hallelujah! I am blessed indeed.

God blesses everything that I set my hand to do. As I learn how to be a faithful person, I know I will always abound with blessings from His hands. I am blessed as I learn to trust Him. I will trust Him with all my heart, without leaning upon my own understanding. In all my ways I will acknowledge Him, and I know He will direct my steps. What a blessing this is for me.

Through God's grace I will keep all His ways. I will listen to His instruction, which gives me wisdom, and I will never refuse it. I will read God's Word, listen to His voice, and watch daily for Him, for I realize that whoever finds Him, finds life and shall obtain His favor.

God gives me the finest of the wheat and He satisfies me with honey from the rock. I will never forget all the Lord's blessings and benefits to me. He forgives all my sins and heals my diseases. He has redeemed my life from the pit and He has satisfied me with good things. My youth is being restored like the eagle's.

As I meditate on God's truth in His Word both day and night, I will always be careful to do what it says. This assures me that I will be both prosperous and successful. I will not forget the Lord's teaching. I will keep His commands in my heart, and I know my years will be prolonged and He will bless me with prosperity.

I am so thankful for all God's blessings in my life.

Related Scriptures: Ephesians 1:3; Proverbs 10:6; Deuteronomy 28:1-9; Psalm 2:12; Proverbs 3:5-6; Proverbs 8:32-35; Psalm 81:16; Psalm 103:1-5; Joshua 1:8; Proverbs 3:1.

Personal Prayer: Thank you, Father, for blessing me so richly in so many ways. You have given so much to me, including the spirit of wisdom and revelation that enables me to know you and your ways more fully. Thank you for the spiritual enlightenment you've given to me. It blesses me to know the hope to which you have called me. Yes, I am blessed indeed, and I love you and praise you for everything. In Jesus' name I pray, Amen.

A Promise to Claim: "The blessing of the Lord, it maketh rich, and he addeth no sorrow with it" (Proverbs 10:22).

Words of Wisdom: *"God's promises are like the stars; the darker the night, the brighter they shine"* (David Nicholas).

6

Blood of Christ

Affirmation of Faith: The blood of Christ cleanses me from all sin—past, present, and future. I am cleansed indeed.

> *In whom we have redemption through his*
> *blood, the forgiveness of sins,*
> *according to the riches of his grace.*

(EPHESIANS 1:7-8)

Central Focus: There is supernatural power in the blood of Jesus Christ. It is the power to save, deliver, forgive, cleanse, and protect. The blood of Jesus Christ that He shed upon the cross for us cleanses us from all sin and enables us to have fellowship with the Father and with one another. His blood is so precious.

Meditation on God's Promises to You: The blood of Jesus Christ purges my conscience from dead works and enables me to serve the living God. I am saved, sanctified, and redeemed by the precious blood of Christ. He is the Lamb of God who was slain from the foundation of the world.

I was not redeemed by corruptible things, such as silver and gold, but with the precious blood of Jesus—the perfect and spotless Lamb of God. His blood is the sacrifice that reconciles me to God, and being reconciled, I will be saved by His life.

I plead the protection of the blood of Jesus Christ over my home and family, and I know God will plant His hedge of protection around us. His blood was shed for the remission of my sins. In the same way that I know I have been justified through His blood, I know I shall be saved from wrath through Him.

Through the blood of Jesus I am able to draw near to the Father. I am able to overcome the enemy through the blood of the Savior and by the word of my testimony. The God of peace who brought Jesus back from the dead through the blood of the everlasting covenant will make me perfect in every good work so that I will always do His will. He will work in me that which is well-pleasing in His sight, through Jesus Christ, to whom be glory forever.

I am washed in the blood of Jesus Christ.

Related Scriptures: Hebrews 9:14; Revelation 13:8; 1 Peter 1:18-19; Romans 5:10; Job 1:10; Matthew 26:28; Romans 5:9; Ephesians 2:13; Revelation 12:11; Hebrews 13:20-21.

Personal Prayer: Loving Father, your covenant with me required that blood be shed for the atonement of my sins. Thank you for commending your love toward me in that while I was yet a sinner, the Lord Jesus Christ shed His blood for me. Because He did so, I am now justified by His blood, and I know I will be saved from the wrath which is to come. I now have redemption and forgiveness of my sins. My future is secure. Thank you for giving me direct access to you through the blood of Jesus. I have spiritual victory and all fear is gone. There is great power in the blood of Jesus. Thank you, Lord. In Jesus' name I pray, Amen.

A Promise to Claim: "But if we walk in the light, as he is in the light, we have fellowship one with another, and the blood of Jesus Christ cleanseth us from all sin" (1 John 1:7).

Words of Wisdom: *"I had a choice: I could believe the lies of the devil, in which case I was on my way to suicide, or I could believe in the promises of God, and be taken through my time of trial"* (Angus Buchan).

7

Burdens

Affirmation of Faith: God is the great Burden-bearer. He bears all my burdens, and I know He cares for me. I release my burdens to the Lord, and I know He will deal with them in the best possible way.

> *Cast thy burden upon the Lord, and he shall sustain thee;*
> *He shall never suffer the righteous to be moved.*

(PSALM 55:22)

Central Focus: Jesus invites you to put your burdens at the foot of the cross. As you do so, you will realize the truth of His promise: "Come unto me, all ye that labour and are heavy laden, and I will give you rest. Take my yoke upon you, and learn of me; for I am meek and lowly in heart, and ye shall find rest for your souls. For my yoke is easy and my burden is light" (Matthew 11:28). Burdens are lifted at Calvary, where the Lord gave His life for you.

Meditation on God's Promises to You: I will obey the Lord and cast all my burdens upon Him. I know He will sustain me as I do so. I enter the rest He has promised to me. My Father is the great burden-bearer. He gives ear to my prayers, and He does not hide from my supplications. He attends to me, and He hears me. He bears my burdens for me and with me.

God has promised to supply all my needs according to His riches in glory by Christ Jesus. My Lord is a shield for me, my glory and the lifter of my head. He hears me, and when I lie down to sleep, I do so peacefully, for I know He sustains me. He is so great to me. He has healed the broken in heart and He has bound up their wounds.

God's power is incomprehensibly great, and His understanding is infinite. I will sing unto Him with great thanksgiving, for He has lifted all my burdens from me. Hallelujah!

Through His grace I will stand fast in the liberty wherewith Christ has set me free, and I will not allow myself to ever get entangled in the enemy's yoke of bondage again. His truth has set me free from all burdens.

God's loving-kindness and truth continually preserve me and lift my burdens from me. The Lord is pleased to deliver me, and He makes haste to help me. Instead of focusing on the burdens of life, I will rejoice and be glad in Him. I will magnify Him and His holy, blessed name.

I waited patiently for the Lord, and He inclined unto me, and heard my cry. He brought me out of a horrible pit and the miry clay. He set my feet upon a rock and established my goings. He has put a new song in my mouth, even praise to Him. Many shall see it and fear and trust in the Lord.

I am blessed because I have made the Lord my trust. I will ever trust Him, because He has taken all burdens from me, and He has given me His glorious peace. Hallelujah!

Related Scriptures: Psalm 55:22; Matthew 11:28; Psalm 55:1-2; Philippians 4:19; Psalm 3; Psalm 147:5-6; Galatians 5:1; John 8:32; Psalm 40:1-4.

Personal Prayer: Dear Lord, I know how blessed I am. I know you care for me and want to help me deal with any burdens. I give all my burdens to you, for I know this is the way to perfect peace and rest. Thank you for being my great burden-bearer and the One who walks alongside me as I journey through life. Even heavy burdens are light when you are helping me. Praise the Lord! In Jesus' name I pray, Amen.

A Promise to Claim: "Cast thy burden on the Lord, and he shall sustain thee: he shall never suffer the righteous to be moved" (Psalm 55:22).

Words of Wisdom: *"When our trials come, when we feel pain and suffering, when our tears flow again, it is our joy and comfort to lift our faces heavenward and to go on, standing on the promises of God"* (W.A. Criswell).

8

Calling

Affirmation of Faith: I am called and chosen by God. I did not choose Him, but He chose me, and I know He chose me to bear much fruit. With His help I will be a fruit-bearing Christian.

> *As ye know how we exhorted and comforted and charged every one*
> *of you, as a father doth his own children, that you would walk worthy*
> *of God who hath called you unto his own kingdom and glory.*

(1 THESSALONIANS 2:11-12).

Central Focus: The word vocation means calling. God has called you out of darkness, into His marvelous light. He has called you to bear much fruit, and your fruit will remain. He has chosen you to do His work on Earth; you did not choose Him. Follow Him each step of the way. What has He called you to do?

Meditation on God's Promises to You: God has called me to liberty, peace, light, and into a personal, intimate relationship with Him. I respond to His call with joy and enthusiasm.

He has sanctified me in Christ Jesus, and He has called me to be a saint along with all who call upon the name of the Lord Jesus Christ. God is faithful to me, and I am so thankful that I have been called into fellowship with Him and with His Son, the Lord Jesus Christ.

He is the power and wisdom of God to me. Hallelujah! I behold my calling with excitement and happiness. God has chosen the foolish things of the world to confound the wise, and He has chosen the weak things of the world to confound those which are mighty. He has also chosen the base things of the world, even those things that are despised, to bring to nothing the things that are. I thank Him that He has called me.

It thrills me to realize that all things work together for good in my life, because I've been called according to my Father's good purpose. My God has called and justified me so that He might make known the riches of His glory unto me.

I will ever abide in the calling that He has extended to me. How I rejoice in the truth that He has called me into the glorious liberty of the children of God. I am called to be His servant, and I assume that responsibility with gratitude and devotion.

I am so thankful that God has called me into the

grace of Christ and into His freedom. I will not use this freedom as an occasion to the flesh, but through love I will serve others. I will walk worthy of the vocation to which I've been called.

My God has called me, and I respond, "Yes, Lord!"

Related Scriptures: 1 Thessalonians 2:12; Romans 1:7; 1 Corinthians 7:15; 1 Peter 2:9; 1 Corinthians 1:9; 1 Corinthians 1:2; 1 Corinthians 1:9; 1 Corinthians 1:24; 1 Corinthians 1:26; 1 Corinthians 1:27-28; Romans 8:28; Romans 8:30; Romans 9:23; 1 Corinthians 7:20; 1 Corinthians 7:21; Romans 8:21; 1 Corinthians 7:22; Galatians 1:15; Galatians 5:13; Ephesians 4:1.

Personal Prayer: Heavenly Father, thank you for calling me, first as your child. You have also called me to be one of your saints. How I thank you for the certain knowledge that you have called me according to your eternal purpose. I am no longer my own. You have bought me, redeemed me, set me free, cleansed me, and delivered me. Hallelujah! In Jesus' name I pray, Amen.

A Promise to Claim: "And let the peace of God rule in your hearts, to the which also ye are called in one body; and be ye thankful. Let the word of Christ dwell in you richly in all wisdom" (Colossians 3:15-16).

Words of Wisdom: *"God never calls His people to accomplish anything without promising to supply their every need"* (Charles R. Swindoll).

9

Commitment

Affirmation of Faith: My commitment to Christ will see me through every situation. I will commit my life afresh to Him each day.

> *Commit thy way unto the Lord; trust also*
> *In him; and he shall bring it to pass. And he*
>   *shall bring forth*
> *thy righteousness as the light, and thy*
>   *judgement as the noonday.*

(PSALM 37:5-7)

Central Focus: God is committed to you. Have you totally committed your life to Him? Remember, commitment is a promise, and He promises to take good care of you. To commit your life to Christ is to give your life to Him. When this happens, you are no longer in charge of your life, your decisions, or your plans, for He is. You have given Him everything that applies to you.

Meditation on God's Promises to You: I commit my life to my Lord Jesus Christ. I will confess Him with my mouth, as I believe in my heart that God has raised Him from the dead. I know I am saved, for with my heart I have believed unto righteousness and with my mouth I have made confession unto salvation. Praise the Lord!

I shall never be ashamed because I believe on Him. He saved me when I called upon Him. I will trust in the Lord and do good. I know He will take care of me and meet all my needs. I delight myself in the Lord, and I know He will give me the desires of my heart as I continue to commit my life to Him.

I commit all my ways to Him, and I trust fully in Him. I know He will answer my prayers. He will bring forth my righteousness as the light and my judgment as the noonday.

I will rest in the Lord and wait patiently for Him. I will not worry about evildoers who prosper. Instead, I will put all my hope in the Lord. I will seek the Lord while He may be found. I will call upon Him while He is near.

I will always believe in the Lord, for I know that without faith it is impossible to please Him, for He that comes to God must believe that He is and that He is a rewarder of all who diligently seek Him. He is leading me, as I grow in grace and in the knowledge of my Lord Jesus Christ. To Him be glory both now and forever.

As I draw near to God, He draws near to me. I cleanse my hands and I purify my heart. I am not ashamed, because I know whom I have believed and I know that He is able to keep that which I've committed unto Him against that day.

I am so thankful that I've committed my life—everything I am and have—to Him!

Related Scriptures: Romans 10:9-13; Psalm 37:3-7; Isaiah 55:6; Hebrews 11:6; 2 Peter 3:9, 18; James 4:8; 2 Timothy 1:12.

Personal Prayer: Lord God, I give my life to you and I commit my ways to you. I know you will always take care of me and watch out for me. Thank you for your commitment to me. I surrender everything I am and have to you, because I know it is yours to begin with. I will not worry or fear. These are my commitments to you, and I thank you for hearing me and helping me. Keep me in the center of your will at all times. In Jesus' name I pray, Amen.

A Promise to Claim: "Trust in the Lord, and do good; so shalt thou dwell in the land, and verily thou shalt be fed. Delight thyself also in the Lord; and he shall give thee the desires of thine heart. Commit thy way unto the Lord; trust also in him; and he shall bring it to pass" (Psalm 37:3-5).

Words of Wisdom: *"It was character that got us out of bed, commitment that moved us into action, and discipline that enabled us to follow through"* (Zig Ziglar).

Confusion

Affirmation of Faith: I will take time to wait on God, and I know He will lift me out of all confusion. I will resist any confusion that enters my mind, for I know it comes from the evil one.

For God is not the author of confusion, but of peace.

(1 CORINTHIANS 14:33)

Central Focus: Never be afraid or confused. God is always there, and He will lift you out of all confusion and doubt. Confusion is the result of failing to ascertain the will of God as it is revealed in the Scriptures. It is a state of disorganization and even bewilderment. Such a condition does not come from God, but its solution is to seek God with all your heart.

Meditation on God's Promises to You: I will trust in the Lord with all my heart and not lean upon my own understanding. In all my ways I will acknowledge Him, and I know He will direct my steps and lead me out of any and all confusion.

I realize that a double-minded person is unstable in all his ways, and this leads to great confusion and bewilderment. I also know that when I lack wisdom, all I need to do is to ask God, and He will impart His wisdom to me. I will do so in faith, with no confusion or double-mindedness at all.

God is guiding me with His eye. He will always instruct me and teach me in the way in which I should go. God has not given me a spirit of fear or confusion, but of love, power, and a sound mind. He is not the author of any confusion.

God is always helping me. Therefore, I will not be disgraced or confused, because I have set my face like a flint and I know I will not be ashamed. Because I have committed my life to Him, I know I will never be confused or ashamed, and I know He will keep what I've committed unto Him.

I love God's Word and this brings great peace to me. As a result, I know that nothing will cause me to stumble or be confused.

I cast all my burdens upon Him, including the burden of confusion, and He is sustaining me. He will never permit me to be moved or to confused as long as I do so. He gives power to me when I am weak, and He increases my strength. Hallelujah!

All confusion is gone from my life. I trust completely in the Lord.

Related Scriptures: Proverbs 3:5-6; James 1:1-8; Psalm 32:8; 2 Timothy 1:7; 1 Corinthians 14:33;

Isaiah 50:7; 2 Timothy 1:12; Psalm 119:165; Psalm 55:22; Isaiah 40:29.

Personal Prayer: Dear Father, help me to recognize the times when confusion comes to me and to confront it with the faith that stems from your holy Word. I refuse to let confusion cloud my mind, and I thank you that you are setting me free from all confusion by giving me a renewed mind that is clear and focused on you. I know I cannot be confused when I am in the center of your will, and I purpose, with your help and through your grace, to stay there. In Jesus' name I pray, Amen.

A Promise to Claim: "For God is not the author of confusion, but of peace, as in all churches of the saints" (1 Corinthians 14:33).

Words of Wisdom: *"Never be in a hurry; do everything quietly and in a calm spirit. Do not lose your inner peace for anything whatsoever, even if your whole world seems upset"* (St. Francis de Sales).

Deliverance

Affirmation of Faith: God has already delivered me, so I will walk in the deliverance He has provided each day of my life.

> *I will love thee, O Lord, my strength. The Lord is my rock,*
> *and my fortress, and my deliverer; my God, my strength,*
> *in whom I will trust; my buckler, and the horn of my salvation,*
> *and my high tower.*

(PSALM 18:1-2)

Central Focus: Jesus is your Deliverer. Deliverance from sin, the devil, and darkness is yours, and your responsibility is to maintain the deliverance God has provided for you. This means that He has the power to set you completely free, rescue you, and release you from the power of Satan and sin. He delivers you from the powers of darkness so you may enter into His glorious light and stay there forever.

Meditation on God's Promises to You: My God is my mighty Deliverer. He tears down strongholds that are erected by the enemy. I will be strong in the Lord and in the power of His might. As I submit myself to God, I will resist the devil, and I know he will flee from me.

The Lord has given me the power to tread on serpents and scorpions and over all the power of the enemy. Praise His holy name! I will be sober and vigilant, because I know my adversary, the devil, as a roaring lion, walks about seeking whom he may devour. Through God's grace, I will steadfastly resist him in the faith.

The Lord will preserve me from all evil. He will preserve my soul. He will preserve my going out and my coming in from this time forth and forevermore. Hallelujah! He is delivering me from the snare of the fowler and from the noisome pestilence. He covers me with His feathers, and under His wings I shall trust. His truth is my shield and buckler.

Because of His delivering power, which is at work in my life, I will not be afraid for the terror by night nor for the arrow that flies by day. A thousand shall fall at my side and 10,000 at my right hand, but I know God will protect me.

The Lord is faithful. He is establishing me, and He is keeping me from evil. The Lord shall deliver me from every evil work, and He will preserve me unto His heavenly kingdom. To Him be glory forever and ever.

I praise God that His deliverance is at work in my life.

Related Scriptures: Ephesians 6:10; James 4:7; Luke 10:19; 1 Peter 5:8-9; Psalm 127:7-8; Psalm 91; 2 Thessalonians 3:3; 2 Timothy 4:18.

Personal Prayer: Father, I come to you in Jesus' name with great gratitude in my heart for the deliverance you have provided for me. Thank you for delivering me from all the power of the enemy and for setting me free. I will walk in the freedom and deliverance you have given to me every step of my way, and I will give the message of deliverance to those I come in contact with. Thank you, Father. In Jesus' name I pray, Amen.

A Promise to Claim: "He hath delivered my soul in peace from the battle that was against me" (Psalm 55:18).

Words of Wisdom: *"The Lord never came to deliver men from the consequences of their sins while yet those sins remained. . . . Yet men, loving their sins and feeling nothing of their own dread hatefulness, have, consistent with their low condition, constantly taken this word concerning the Lord to mean that He came to save them from the punishment of their sins"* (George MacDonald).

Discouragement

Affirmation of Faith: The opposite of discourage-ment is encouragement. I will encourage myself in God and His Word. Thereby I will not be discouraged.

> Though I walk in the midst of trouble, thou
>   wilt revive me;
> thou shalt stretch forth thine hand against
>   the wrath of mine enemies,
> and thy hand shall save me.

(PSALM 138:7)

Central Focus: Feelings are not your master, circumstances are not your Lord, and emotions are not your guide. Essentially, discouragement stems from a lack of courage. To overcome discouragement, continue to encourage yourself in the Lord by meditating upon His Word every day. Wait for the Lord and walk in His presence, for in His presence there is abundant joy.

Meditation on God's Promises to You: There is no reason for me to be discouraged. I will not cast away my confidence, which has great reward. I know I have need of endurance, so that after I have done the will of God, I may receive the promise.

Jesus has given me His peace, not as the world gives. Therefore, I will not permit my heart ever to be troubled, to be afraid, or to be discouraged. Like Paul, even when I am hard-pressed on every side, I am not crushed. Even though I might be perplexed at times, I will never despair. When I am persecuted, I will realize that I am not forsaken.

I am confident of this very thing: that He who has begun a good work in me, will complete it until the day of Christ. The Lord is my light and salvation. Whom shall I fear? The Lord is the strength of my life. Of whom shall I be afraid? Though an army might encamp against me, my heart shall not fear. In this I will be confident: my head shall be lifted up above my enemies all around me; therefore, I will offer sacrifices of joy in His tabernacle. I will sing praises to the Lord and not be discouraged.

With God's help, I will be of good courage. I know He will strengthen my heart, as I hope in Him. The genuineness of my faith, being much more precious than gold that perishes, though it be tested by fire, may be found to praise, honor, and glory at the revelation of Jesus Christ. Even though I have not seen Him, I love Him. Believing, I rejoice with inexpressible joy that is full of glory, receiving the end of my faith—the salvation of my soul.

I refuse to be discouraged because the Lord has ransomed me. I come to Zion with singing and with everlasting joy upon my head. I have obtained joy and gladness, and all sorrow, sighing, and discouragement have fled away.

The joy of the Lord is my strength.

Related Scriptures: Hebrews 10:35-36; John 14:27; 2 Corinthians 4:8-9; Philippians 1:6; Psalm 27:1-3, 6; Psalm 31:24; 1 Peter 1:6-9; Isaiah 51:11; Nehemiah 8:10.

Personal Prayer: Heavenly Father, I ask for confidence and courage that will keep me from ever being discouraged. Help me to remember to encourage myself in you and to stand fast at all times. Help me to be an encourager to others, for in this world it seems that so many are discouraged. I want to remind them of your love and salvation, for in these there is no room for discouragement. Thank you for keeping me from all discouragement, dear Lord. In Jesus' name I pray, Amen.

A Promise to Claim: "Being confident of this very thing, that he which hath begun a good work in you will perform it until the day of Jesus Christ" (Philippians 1:6).

Words of Wisdom: *"True silence is the rest of the mind; it is to the spirit what sleep is to the body, nourishment and refreshment"* (William Penn).

Envy

Affirmation of Faith: Envy and jealousy have no place in a believer's life. God is keeping me from all forms of envy, covetousness, and jealousy.

> *For where envying and strife is, there is confusion and every evil work.*

(JAMES 3:16)

Central Focus: Envy is one of the Seven Deadly Sins, and covetousness is strictly forbidden by the Ten Commandments. Instead of envying others, endeavor to express gratitude to God for them and for all they have. Envy will lead you to become discontented with your own lot, and it involves feelings of resentment and ill will toward others. There can be no place for envy in your life, because God wants you to love others and to rejoice with them.

Meditation on God's Promises to You: Whenever I feel envy rising within me, I must confess it to God. As I do so, He forgives me and cleanses me from all unrighteousness. His Word tells me that a sound heart is the life of the flesh, but envy is rottenness in my bones. I want a sound heart, so I will avoid envy at all times by being content in whatever state I find myself.

Envy often stems from pride, arguing, and strife, so, with God's help, I will avoid these sins as well. It is the desire of my heart to walk honestly, not in strife and envy. I will put on the Lord Jesus Christ and make no provision for my flesh.

They who are after the flesh do mind the things of the flesh, but they that are after the Spirit the things of the Spirit. Therefore, I will be spiritually minded, not carnally minded, because spiritual mindedness leads to life and peace, whereas carnal mindedness leads to spiritual death.

Through God's grace I no longer have any desire for vainglory, and I do not want to provoke others or be envious of them. Instead, I want to be wise and to show forth the works of the Lord in meekness instead of living in the bitterness of envy and strife.

I will walk in the Spirit so as not to fulfill the lusts of my flesh. The Spirit of life in Christ Jesus has set me free from the law of sin and death. I choose, therefore, to mortify envy and all misdeeds of my body and soul. I will be led by God's Spirit.

God has delivered me from the sin of envy. Praise His holy name!

Related Scriptures: 1 John 1:9; Proverbs 14:30; 1 Timothy 6:4; Romans 13:13; Romans 13:14; Romans 8:5-6; Romans 8:2; Romans 8:13-14.

Personal Prayer: Dear Father in Heaven, I thank you for your Word, which shows me clearly how you want me to live. I will walk in the light of your Word and rise above all envy of others. Thank you for making me a special child of yours. You have called me and you have befriended me. Because I know these things are true, I know there is no place for envy in my life. Help me to mind my own business and to owe no person anything except to love them. In Jesus' name I pray, Amen.

A Promise to Claim: "Charity suffereth long, and is kind; charity envieth not; charity vaunteth not itself, is not puffed up, doth not behave itself unseemly, seeketh not her own, is not easily provoked, thinketh no evil; rejoiceth not in iniquity, but rejoiceth in the truth; beareth all things, believeth all things, hopeth all things, endureth all things. Charity never faileth" (1 Corinthians 13:4-7).

Words of Wisdom: *"Never underestimate the power of jealousy and the power of envy to destroy. Never underestimate that"* (Oliver Stone).

Eternal Life

Affirmation of Faith: Eternal life is here and now, and it will never end. Through Jesus I know I have everlasting life.

> *For God so loved the world, that he gave his only begotten Son,*
> *that whosoever believeth in him should not perish, but have everlasting life.*

(JOHN 3:16)

Central Focus: God's gift is eternal life, and He will always be there for you, even throughout all eternity. The death of Jesus Christ on the cross opens the door to eternal life for us, and His resurrection from the dead assures us that we will live with Him forever. Someone has put it this way: the unbeliever is born once and dies twice, but the true believer is born twice and dies once.

Meditation on God's Promises to You: As I meditate upon God's Word and believe in Jesus Christ, I will not be condemned nor will I perish, but I will pass from death to life. I confess with my mouth the Lord Jesus, and I believe in my heart that God has raised Him from the dead. Therefore, I know I have eternal life.

Because I am in Christ, I am a new creation. Old things are passed away, and all things have become new to me. I am crucified with Christ. Nevertheless, I live. Yet, not I, but Christ lives in me. And the life I now live in the flesh I live by the faith of the Son of God who loved me and gave himself for me. I have been born again by the Word of God, which lives and abides forever.

How I thank God that He has given me eternal life, and this life is in His Son, and it has already begun! I believe in Him. Therefore, I have eternal life. Hallelujah! Because Jesus is the living bread which came down from Heaven and I have partaken of that bread, I know I will live forever.

Surely goodness and mercy shall follow me all the days of my life, and I will dwell in the house of the Lord forever! I am His sheep and I hear His voice speaking to me. I will follow Him, and He will give me eternal life. Therefore, I shall never perish, and no one shall ever be able to snatch me out of His hand.

To know that I have eternal life is a blessed assurance.

Related Scriptures: John 5:24; Romans 10:9; 2 Corinthians 5:17; Galatians 2:20; 1 Peter 1:23; 1 John 5:11; John 6:47; John 6:51; Psalm 23:6; John 10:27-28.

Personal Prayer: Heavenly Father, I thank you so much for sending Jesus to die for me on the cross. Because He did so, I know I have everlasting life. Because He lives, I can become a prevailing warrior in your Kingdom. I thank you that Jesus is preparing a place for me so that I can be with Him forever. He is my Lord and Savior, and He is the King of kings and Lord of lords. It is my honor and my pleasure to serve Him in every way I can. Thank you for your everlasting love, Lord God. In Jesus' name I pray, Amen.

A Promise to Claim: "For God so loved the world, that he gave his only begotten Son, that whosoever believeth in him should not perish, but have everlasting [eternal] life" (John 3:16).

Words of Wisdom: *"I want to know one thing: the way to Heaven. God himself has condescended to teach me the way. He has written it down in a book. Oh, give me that book! At any price give me the book of God. Let me be a man of one book"* (John Wesley).

Faith

Affirmation of Faith: Faith is the key to believing and receiving God's promises. Through faith I have the victory that overcomes the world.

> *But without faith it is impossible to please*
> *him: for he that cometh to God must*
> *believe that he is, and that he is a rewarder*
> *of them that diligently seek him.*

(HEBREWS 11:6)

Central Focus: Faith enables you to prevail in any and all circumstances. It leads you to become more than a conqueror, for "Faith is the victory that overcomes the world." (See 1 John 5:4.) It is through faith in God's promises that you are able to prevail in life. God is faithful, which means He is full of faith, and you can be too.

Meditation on God's Promises to You: Faith is the substance of things hope for, the evidence of things not seen. The trial of my faith is more precious than of gold that perishes, though it be tried by fire. I believe it will be found unto praise and honor and glory at the appearing of Jesus Christ. I love Him even though I haven't seen Him, and I rejoice with joy unspeakable and full of glory.

I have been justified by Christ, and I shall live by His faith. Faith comes by hearing and hearing by the Word of God. Therefore, I will spend much time in God's Word, meditating upon its truths and learning the ways of Christ. Enlighten me as I study your Word. Let the Word of God fill me with all wisdom.

I know that with God nothing shall ever be impossible. I will be strong in faith, giving glory to God, because I know that God is able to perform what He promises to me. Hallelujah! I will walk by faith and not by sight.

I believe the promise of Jesus which states that all things are possible to one who believes. Absolutely nothing is too hard for God.

I will walk in victory, for I know that faith is the victory that overcomes the world.

Related Scriptures: Hebrews 11:1; 1 Peter 1:7-8; Romans 1:17; Romans 10:17; Luke 1:37; Romans 4:20-21; 2 Corinthians 5:7; Mark 9:23; Jeremiah 32:27; 1 John 5:4.

Personal Prayer: Abba Father, I take my stand upon your powerful Word and all the promises it contains. I will put on your full armor, which includes truth, the breastplate of righteousness, the gospel of peace, the shield of faith, the helmet of salvation, the sword of the Spirt (the Word of God), and prayer. I receive your promises, believe your promises, and share your promises with others. Thank you so much for the gift of faith, which is at work in my life. In Jesus' name I pray, Amen.

A Promise to Claim: "That the trial of your faith, being much more precious than of gold that perisheth, though it be tried with fire, might be found unto praise and honour and glory at the appearing of Jesus Christ: whom having not seen, ye love; in whom, though now ye see him not, yet believing, ye rejoice with joy unspeakable and full of glory: receiving the end of your faith, even the salvation of your souls" (1 Peter 1:7-9).

Words of Wisdom: *"When thou prayest, rather let thy heart be without words than thy words without heart"* (John Bunyan).

16

Fear

Affirmation of Faith: There is no fear in God's love. I am free from the fear of the future. I am free indeed.

For God hath not given us the spirit of fear;
but of power, and of love,
and of a sound mind.

(2 TIMOTHY 1:7)

Central Focus: Fear crumbles in front of the fortress of faith. God's perfect love casts out all fear from our lives. (See 1 John 4:18.) There is, therefore, no room for fear in a believer's heart. All fear is gone because of the blood of Christ. There is absolutely nothing to be afraid of, for you already know the end of the story. God sees your life from beginning to end, and He is always watching out for you.

Meditation on God's Promises to You: God has adopted me into His family. I did not receive the spirit of bondage again to fear, but I have received the spirit of adoption by whom I am able to cry out, "Abba, Father!"

He covers me with His feathers, and under His wings I take refuge. His truth is my shield and my buckler. I will not be afraid of anything. He is giving His angels charge over me, to keep me in all my ways. I will fear no evil.

God is my light and my salvation, and because this is true, I will fear no person or thing. He is the stronghold of my life. Hallelujah! Knowing that He is with me, what can man do to me? I am so thankful that my heavenly Father has not given me a spirit of fear, but one of love, power, and self-discipline. I will walk in His love, power, and self-control every step of my way.

He is my help and my shield. His love is always with me, from everlasting to everlasting. Therefore, I will be strong and courageous at all times. I will not be afraid or terrified by anything, for I know He will never leave me nor forsake me.

There is no fear in God's love. Indeed, His perfect love casts out all fear from me. Because I know this is true, I will never fear again. He is keeping me in perfect peace, as I learn to keep my mind stayed on Him.

I will trust in Him with all my heart, without leaning upon my own understanding. In all my ways I will acknowledge Him, and I know He will direct my steps.

There is no reason to fear whatsoever!

Related Scriptures: Romans 8:15; Psalm 91; Psalm 23:4; Psalm 27:1; 2 Timothy 1:7; Psalm 115:11;

Psalm 103:17; Deuteronomy 31:6; 1 Chronicles 28:20; 1 John 4:18; Isaiah 26:3; Proverbs 3:5-6.

Personal Prayer: Dear Lord, thank you for delivering me from all fear, anxiety, and worry. I now know that I have nothing to be afraid of. Your Word declares peace to me. Therefore, I will fear nothing, including other people. I thank you that you have freed me from fear through your perfect love. I love you, Father. In Jesus' name I pray, Amen.

A Promise to Claim: "There is no fear in love; but perfect love casteth out fear: because fear hath torment. He that feareth is not made perfect in love" (1 John 4:18).

Words of Wisdom: *"Those who have steeped their souls in prayer can every anguish bear"* (Richard Monckton Milnes).

17

Forgiveness

Affirmation of Faith: You are forgiven by God, so make it a priority to forgive others. Through forgiveness relationships are restored, strengthened, and deepened.

If we confess our sins, he is faithful and just
*   to forgive us our sins,*
and to cleanse us from all unrighteousness.

(1 JOHN 1:9)

Central Focus: There are at least four aspects of forgiveness that we need in our lives. To be forgiven by God and others. To forgive others, and to forgive ourselves. We know that God is willing to forgive us when we confess our sins to Him. Forgiveness is the only solution to some of the problems we experience with other people. It is as we are forgiven (and forgive ourselves), that we are able to forgive those who have wronged us. God wants you to learn to forgive others in the same way that He has forgiven you. As you do so, deep and abiding changes take place in all your relationships.

Meditation on God's Promises to You: Because I have confessed my sins to Him, I know that God has forgiven me and cleansed me from all unrighteousness. The blood of Jesus Christ, His Son, has cleansed me from all sin—past, present, and future. I am very grateful for the power of His blood in my life and for the forgiveness that God has extended to me.

I wait for Him, and in His Word do I hope. My loving Father has opened my eyes, turned me from darkness to light and from the power of Satan. He has given His power to me so that I would receive His forgiveness and all of His wonderful inheritance. I praise Him for sanctifying me by faith.

Blessed be the God and Father of my Lord Jesus Christ, who has blessed me with all spiritual blessings in heavenly places in Christ. According as He has chosen me in Him before the foundation of the world, that I would be holy and without blame before Him in love.

I give thanks to the Father who has made me a partaker of the inheritance of the saints in light. He has delivered me from the power of darkness and has translated me into the Kingdom of His dear Son in whom I have redemption through His blood, even the forgiveness of sins.

It is my heart's desire to be kind to others, tender-hearted, and forgiving, even as God for Christ's sake has forgiven me. I will be a follower of God and walk in love, as Christ also has loved me and has given himself as an offering and sacrifice to God.

I am so thankful that God has forgiven me. Now I will endeavor to forgive others and myself.

Related Scriptures: 1 John 1:9; 1 John 1:7; Psalm 130:4-5; Acts 26:8; Colossians 1:12-14; Ephesians 4:29-5:1.

Personal Prayer: Father, thank you for forgiving me through the blood of your Son, Jesus Christ. Your Word is so precious to me, and I will walk in the light it provides each step of my way. Through your grace I now choose to forgive everyone who has wronged me in any way. Thank you for your grace, which enables me to walk in forgiveness and love. In the precious name of Jesus I pray, Amen.

A Promise to Claim: "If we confess our sins, he is faithful and just to forgive us our sins, and to cleanse us from all unrighteousness" (1 John 1:9).

Words of Wisdom: *"Settle yourself in solitude, and you will come upon Him in yourself"* (Saint Theresa).

18

Freedom

Affirmation of Faith: Christ died to set you free from sin and Satan. You are free indeed.

And ye shall know the truth, and the truth shall make you free.

(JOHN 8:32)

Central Focus: The Lord has set you free so you would be free indeed. Your responsibility is to stand fast in that liberty and to be certain that you are never again entangled with that yoke of bondage. (See Galatians 5:1.) You are free from the fear of the future and the guilt of the past.

Meditation on God's Promises to You: Jesus Christ is the way, the truth, and the life, and it is through Him that I am able to find spiritual freedom. I am now free indeed. Hallelujah! Thank God for this precious freedom. I used to be a servant of sin, but now I am free from all sin, and I've become a servant of righteousness.

As a result, I yield all of my life and every part of my body to serve righteousness unto holiness. There is, therefore, no condemnation to me, because I am in Christ Jesus, and I walk not after the flesh, but after the Spirit. The law of the Spirit of life in Christ Jesus has set me free from the law of sin and death.

My Father has delivered me from the bondage of corruption, and I have entered into the glorious liberty of the sons of God. The Lord is that Spirit, and where the Spirit of the Lord is, there is liberty. I will walk in the Spirit and in His liberty each step of my way.

I will continue to look into the perfect law of liberty. I will not be a forgetful hearer of God's Word. I will be a doer of God's Word, and I will spend time in His Word every day, for I realize this will help me to maintain my liberty in Him.

According to Christ's divine power He has given unto me all things that pertain to life and godliness, including spiritual freedom. He has given me His great and precious promises, that by these I would be a partaker of the divine nature, having escaped the world and all its lusts.

God has called me to follow in the steps of Christ. I will learn from His example and endeavor to do what I know He would do. He did not sin, and no guile could be found within Him. He has enabled me to die to sin and to be alive to righteousness. This is true spiritual freedom.

I truly am free from the guilt of the past and the fear of the future. Hallelujah!

Related Scriptures: John 14:6; Romans 6:18-19; Romans 8:1-2; Galatians 5:13-16; James 1:25; 2 Peter 1:3-4; 1 Peter 2:21-24.

Personal Prayer: Lord God, the freedom you've given to me is very precious indeed. It has removed all my fears, anxieties, and worries. Hallelujah! Thank you for justifying me freely by your grace through the redemption that your Son, Jesus Christ, has provided for me. It is this that enables me to enter into the glorious liberty of your children—a glorious liberty indeed. From this time forward, I will walk in spiritual freedom. In Jesus' name I pray, Amen.

A Promise to Claim: "If the Son therefore shall make you free, ye shall be free indeed" (John 8:36).

Words of Wisdom: *"There are two ways to live your life. One is as though nothing is a miracle. The other is as though everything is a miracle"* (Albert Einstein).

19

Gladness and Joy

Affirmation of Faith: I will let the Lord's gladness and joy fill my soul. In this I know I will find true joy—the joy of the Lord.

*Thou hast put gladness in my heart, more
than in the time that*
their corn and their wine increased.

(PSALM 4:7)

Central Focus: Are you glad in the Lord? Do you realize that His joy is your strength? He does want you to know Him in all His fullness and to be glad in Him. In His presence there is fullness of joy and there are pleasures forevermore. (See Psalm 16:11.) True happiness is the joy of the Lord. It is not based on external events or circumstances, but it stems from His presence within you.

Meditation on God's Promises to You: God has put gladness into my heart. He is my helper, and He has turned my mourning into dancing. I rejoice in the truth that He has girded me with gladness, to the end that my glory will sing praise to Him and not be silent. I will give thanks to the Lord forever.

Jesus wants my joy to be full. That's why He shared His heart with us through the Word and His wonderful promises. He knows that if we learn to love Him and others, our joy will be full. I rejoice as I place all my trust in Him, and I will ever shout for joy because He defends me.

The Kingdom of God is not meat and drink, but it is righteousness, peace, and joy in the Holy Ghost. My heart is merry, and this does me good like a medicine.

This is the day the Lord has made. I will rejoice and be glad in it. Hallelujah for this day! God's Word is the joy and rejoicing of my heart, for I am called by the name of the Lord. I will rejoice in Him, and I will joy in Him.

My joy is made complete when I pray in the authority of Jesus' name. God hears and answers my prayers. Hallelujah! His joy goes so much deeper than anything this world has to offer. Like a fountain that springs from the depths of the Earth, the joy of the Lord bubbles up from my spirit and fills me. Then it flows forth from my life and touches all those with whom I come in contact.

This precious joy is a gift from my heavenly Father who loves me with an everlasting love. The joy He gives to me is truly inexpressible; it is full of His glory. His joy enables me to rise above the circumstances of my life and to stay on top.

As I enter and experience His presence, my heart is overcome with joy. He pours His joy upon me, and it overflows in all areas of my life. It covers me and reaches out to others. How I rejoice in His marvelous love for me, which gives me joy and gladness all the time.

I will walk in joy and gladness with the Lord.

Related Scriptures: Psalm 4:7; Psalm 30:11-12; John 15:11-12; Psalm 51:11; Romans 14:17; Proverbs 17:22; Psalm 118:24; Jeremiah 15:16; John 16:24; John 16:23; Psalm 43:4; Isaiah 55:12; Psalm 106:1; 1 Peter 1:8; Psalm 126; Psalm 16:11; Hebrews 1:9; Ephesians 2:4.

Personal Prayer: God of all gladness, thank you for your joy which bubbles up within my soul from the inner wellspring that comes from knowing you. It floods my spirit, soul, and body. Thank you, Father, for filling my mind and my heart with happiness. It causes me to sing for joy as I realize who you are and when I contemplate all you have done for me. You are my highest joy and my complete delight. I will walk in the strength of your joy each step of my way, and I know my joy will be full. In Jesus' joyful name I pray, Amen.

A Promise to Claim: "Thou has loved righteousness and hated iniquity; therefore God, even thy God, hath anointed thee with the oil of gladness above thy fellows" (Hebrews 1:9).

Words of Wisdom: *"Joy is increased by spreading it to others"* (Robert Murray McCheyne).

119

Grace

Affirmation of Faith: Grace enables me to be what I could not be and to do what I could not do. It is unmerited favor and blessing in my life. How thankful I am that God's favor rests upon me.

> *For the Lord God is a sun and shield: the Lord will*
> *give grace and glory: no good thing will he withhold*
> *from them that walk uprightly. O Lord of hosts, blessed*
> *is the man that trusteth in thee.*

(PSALM 84:11-12)

Central Focus: It is God's grace that saves you, keeps you, and meets your every need. Though you do not deserve His grace, He continues to surround you with it and with His favor. God's amazing grace is one of the greatest resources of your life. Grace is your enabler, which allows you to do so many things you cannot do on your own. Grace is so much more than just His "unmerited favor." It is His love, mercy, favor, and full blessing in your life. His grace is greater than all your sin, and it is all-sufficient for you.

Meditation on God's Promises to You: Great grace is upon me, and God's grace enables me to find favor and high esteem in the sight of God and man. God has blessed me so much, and His favor surrounds me like a shield.

I pray that God's grace in my life, having spread to so many, will cause thanksgiving to abound to the glory of God. I am so thankful that He has made me accepted in the Beloved to the praise of the glory of His grace. It is with great confidence that I come to God's throne of grace, there to obtain mercy and find grace to help in my times of need.

God's grace is sufficient for me, and His strength is made perfect in my weakness. By His grace, through faith, I was saved. My Savior is Jesus Christ—the incarnate Word of God who is full of grace and truth. He is the way, the truth, and the life.

How thankful I am that I have been justified freely by His grace. His abundant grace in my life provides me with righteousness that enables me to reign in this life with Him. God is making all grace abound to me so that I will always have all sufficiency in all things and be able to accomplish many good works. This is my heart's desire.

The riches of His grace have supplied all my needs. God is so gracious to me. He is always ready to pardon. He is full of mercy and grace. This is my

God. He has always dealt bountifully with me. He delivered my soul from death, my eyes from tears, and my feet from falling.

I am truly privileged to be a partaker of God's abounding grace. The wonderful grace of my loving Lord keeps me. Hallelujah!

Related Scriptures: Acts 4:33; Proverbs 3:4; Psalm 5:12; 2 Corinthians 4:15; Ephesians 1:6; Hebrews 4:16; 2 Corinthians 12:9; Ephesians 2:8; John 1:14; John 14:6; Romans 3:24; Romans 5:17; 2 Corinthians 9:8; Philippians 4:19; Exodus 34:6; Nehemiah 9;17; Psalm 116:7; Psalm 116:8; Ephesians 1:7-8.

Personal Prayer: O Lord, my gracious God, I thank you for your grace which is greater than all my sin. I thank you that it is through your grace that I know that all your promises are for me. I will abound in your grace which is always sufficient for me. I receive the promise of your grace in my life as I pray. I know it is a gift that I cannot earn, but I simply receive it because I know you love me and have given it to me. In Jesus' name I pray, Amen.

A Promise to Claim: "Wherefore we receiving a kingdom which cannot be moved, let us have grace, whereby we may serve God acceptably with reverence and godly fear" (Hebrews 12:28).

Words of Wisdom: *"Happy is the person who has learned the secret of coming to God daily in prayer. Fifteen minutes alone with God every morning can change our outlooks and recharge our batteries"* (Billy Graham).

Healing

Affirmation of Faith: Jesus is the Great Physician, and I believe He wants me to walk in divine health.

> *Bless the Lord, O my soul: and all that is within me, bless his holy name.*
> *Bless the Lord, O my soul, and forget not all his benefits: Who forgiveth*
> *all thine iniquities; who healeth all thy diseases.*

(PSALM 103:1-3)

Central Focus: All healing comes from God. Jesus is the Great Physician, and He is the Healer of our souls and bodies. He wants you to walk in divine health. All healing is a gift from God, and His healing power is available to every believer. Believe and receive His prevailing promises regarding healing.

Meditation on God's Promises to You: Jesus went about doing good and healing all who were oppressed by the devil. He is the same yesterday, today, and forever. He forgives all my sins and He heals all my diseases. He has set me free.

It is He who heals me when I am sick. He took my infirmities and bore my sicknesses. By His stripes I am healed. I believe He wants me to prosper and to be in good health, for I know He sends forth His Word and heals me. Hallelujah!

He has made me whole, and I am complete in Him. I have found completion in Him. He is the God in whom I live, move, and have my being. He has risen with healing in His wings, and He has promised good health to me.

As I wait upon the Lord, my strength renews and I mount up with wings as an eagle does. He makes my heart merry, and this does me good like a medicine. He quickens me by the power of His Holy Spirit within me.

I thank God for the resurrection power of Christ that is within me. He is able to do exceeding abundantly above all that I ask or think, according to the power that works within me. I thank God for the Lord who is the healing Balm of Gilead who brings health to me.

I will ever give attention to the Word of God and incline my ear to God's sayings. I will not let them depart from my eyes. I will keep them in the midst of my heart, for they are life to me and they are health to all my flesh.

I will walk in health and wholeness through the power of Jesus Christ.

Related Scriptures: Acts 10:38; Hebrews 13:8; Psalm 103:3; Galatians 5:1; Exodus 15:26; Matthew

8:17; Isaiah 53:5; 3 John 2; Psalm 107:20; John 15:5; Colossians 2:10; Acts 17:28; Malachi 4:2; 3 John 2; Isaiah 40:31; Proverbs 17:22; Romans 8:11; Philippians 3:10; Ephesians 3:20; Jeremiah 8:22; Proverbs 4:20-22.

Personal Prayer: Lord God, you are my Healer. I truly believe that all healing comes from you. Thank you for enabling me to believe in your healing power. Help me always to remember that the sufferings of this present time are not worthy to be compared to the glory you will reveal to me. I believe in all the promises of your Word, which declare healing of my soul, body, and spirit. Your Holy Spirit is quickening my mortal body as I pray and I will arise to walk in newness of life. In the name of the Great Physician I pray, Amen.

A Promise to Claim: "Is any sick among you? Let him call for the elders of the church; and let them pray over him, anointing him with oil in the name of the Lord: And the prayer of faith shall save the sick, and the Lord shall raise him up; and if he have committed sins, they shall be forgiven him" (James 5:14-15).

Words of Wisdom: *"What a friend we have in Jesus, all our sins and griefs to bear. What a privilege to carry everything to God in prayer"* (Joseph Scriven).

22

Heaven

Affirmation of Faith: Jesus is preparing a place for me in Heaven. I will let the promise of Heaven fill my heart with expectation, wonder, and joy.

> *For we know that if our earthly house of this tabernacle*
> *were dissolved, we have a building of God, an house not made*
> *with hands, eternal in the heavens.*

(2 CORINTHIANS 5:1)

Central Focus: Jesus is preparing a place for us in Heaven. He promises to come again and receive us unto himself so that where He is, we may be also. Our home is in Heaven, and it is an everlasting home. Hallelujah!

Meditation on God's Promises to You: In my Father's house there are many mansions, and Jesus is preparing a home for me there. I look forward to my heavenly home. God's throne is established in Heaven, and Jesus sits at His right hand, ever living to make intercession for me and all believers.

God's Word assures me that my Father is the high and lofty One who inhabits eternity. I am thrilled to know that Heaven is God's throne and the Earth is His footstool. Therefore, I look unto my heavenly Father and I lift up my hands and heart to Him.

The Lord's Prayer shows me how to pray. Hallowed be the name of my Father in Heaven. May His kingdom come and His will be done on Earth as it is in Heaven. The river of the water of life emanates from the Father's throne in Heaven. It is as clear as crystal and so refreshing and cleansing in its power. I desire to bathe in that glorious river.

The house that is being prepared for me in Heaven is not made with human hands, but it is eternal in the heavens. God's Word is filled with promises of eternal life in Heaven, and I look for and long for the Savior, the Lord Jesus Christ, who will change my body into a body that is fashioned like unto His glorious body, according to the working whereby He is able even to subdue all things unto himself.

The Father has made it possible for me to partake of the inheritance of the saints in light, and He has delivered me from the power of darkness and has translated me into the Kingdom of His dear Son. Praise His matchless name!

In Him I have redemption through His blood, even the forgiveness of my sins. He is the image of the invisible God, the firstborn of every creature. By Him were all things created that are in Heaven and that are in Earth, visible and invisible. All things were created by Him and for Him, including me.

Because I know that Heaven is my eternal home, I will not cast away my confidence, which has great reward. I am so thankful for the better and heavenly country the Lord is preparing for me. I look forward to entering the eternal city.

Heaven will be so much better than Earth.

Related Scriptures: John 14:2; Psalm 103:19; Hebrews 7:25; Isaiah 57:15; Isaiah 66:1; Matthew 6:9-10; Revelation 22:1-5; 2 Corinthians 5:1; Philippians 3:20-21; Colossians 1:12-13; Colossians 1:14-16; Hebrews 11:16.

Personal Prayer: Dear Father, thank you for Heaven. I am so happy to know that this world is not my home, but Heaven is. Thank you for the promise of eternal life—a prevailing promise indeed. I look forward to that day when I will be present with you, and I will join with Jesus in worshiping and adoring your forever. What a blessed time that will be. Thank you for the crown of life that you have reserved for me in Heaven. In Jesus' name I pray, Amen.

A Promise to Claim: "Blessed be the God and Father of our Lord Jesus Christ, which according to his abundant mercy hath begotten us again unto a lively hope by the resurrection of Jesus Christ from the dead, to an inheritance incorruptible, and undefiled, and that fadeth not away, reserved in heaven for you, who are kept by the power of God through faith unto salvation ready to be revealed in the last time" (1 Peter 1:3-4).

Words of Wisdom: *"Earth has no sorrow that Heaven cannot heal"* (Thomas More).

23

Holiness

Affirmation of Faith: Holiness is a way of life for those who want to serve God. He has made it possible for me to be holy as He is holy. It is my desire to walk in holiness for the rest of my life.

> *For I am the Lord your God: ye shall*
> *   therefore sanctify*
> *yourselves, and ye shall be holy; for I*
> *   am holy.*

(LEVITICUS 11:44)

Central Focus: God is the Holy One. The only way we can obtain holiness is by being close to Him. We must walk in His holiness, not in any attempt to be holy in ourselves. Without Him, we can do nothing. (See John 15:5.) Let God's holiness lead you into true worship and freedom. Walk in His holiness, and do not try and manufacture your own.

Meditation on God's Promises to You: It is my desire to worship the Lord in the beauty of holiness and to be holy as He is holy. Through God's grace I will make every effort to live in peace with all people and to be holy, for I know that without holiness I shall not be able to see the Lord.

God has chosen me as one of His holy and beloved children. Therefore, I will clothe myself with compassion, kindness, humility, gentleness, and patience. I will forgive others and put on love, which is the perfect bond of unity. I will let the peace of Christ rule in my heart, and I will be thankful.

The great God of peace is sanctifying me thoroughly so that my entire body, soul, and spirit, will be kept blameless and holy at the coming of the Lord Jesus Christ. God is sanctifying (making me holy) through the work of the Holy Spirit and my belief in the truth.

I will pursue righteousness, holiness, faith, love, and peace along with all those who call on the Lord out of a pure heart. I will add goodness to my faith, knowledge to my goodness, self-control to my knowledge, perseverance and godliness to my self-control, brotherly kindness to my goodness, and love to my brotherly kindness.

My body is the temple of the Holy Spirit, who is within me. I have received Him within me. Therefore, I am not my own; I was bought with the price of Christ's shed blood. From this point on I will honor the Lord with my body, soul, and spirit.

Whatever I do, whether eating or drinking or anything else, I will do all for the glory of my Father in Heaven. I will put to death everything that belongs to my earthly nature: sexual immorality, impurity, lust, evil desires, and greed. I renounce all forms of idolatry.

Related Scriptures: Psalm 29:2; 1 Peter 1:15; Colossians 3:12-15; 1 Thessalonians 5:23; 2 Thessalonians 2:13; 2 Timothy 2:22; 2 Peter 1:5-7; 1 Corinthians 6:19; 1 Corinthians 10:31; Colossians 3:25.

Personal Prayer: Help me, holy Father, to learn to be holy as you are holy. I want to walk in your holiness throughout my life. Thank you for imparting your righteousness to me so that I could be holy. In holiness I find happiness and purpose for my life, and it brings wholeness to me. Help me, Lord God, to find holiness in and through you. In Jesus' name I pray, Amen.

A Promise to Claim: "The oath which he sware to our father Abraham, that he would grant unto us, that we being delivered out of the hand of our enemies might serve him without fear, in holiness and righteousness before him, all the days of our life" (Luke 1:73-75).

Words of Wisdom: *"Though no one can go back and make a brand-new start, anyone can start from now and make a brand-new beginning"* (Carl Bard).

Holy Spirit

Affirmation of Faith: The Holy Spirit is my comforter, counselor, helper, and guide.

> *And hope maketh not ashamed, because the love of God is*
> *shed abroad in our hearts by the Holy Ghost which is given unto us.*

(ROMANS 5:5)

Central Focus: We are the temple of the Holy Spirit who gives us the power to witness, be victorious, live fully, and to deny all worldly lusts and attractions. He lives within us and He quickens our mortal bodies. As He fills us, we become fruitful. We learn to bear His fruit in our lives—love, joy, peace, patience, gentleness, goodness, faith, meekness, and self-control. Be filled with the Holy Spirit.

Meditation on God's Promises to You: My body is the temple of the Holy Spirit. He lives within me. Therefore, I am no longer my own in any way, because I belong to Him. The Holy Spirit is always my Helper. God sent Him to me, and He will abide with me forever. He is the Spirit of truth. The world cannot receive Him, because it neither sees Him nor knows Him. However, I know Him, for He dwells with me and within me.

I choose to be filled with the Holy Spirit. He is guiding me into all truth and He is telling me of things to come. The Holy Spirit does not speak of himself, but of the Lord Jesus Christ. He always glorifies Jesus, and I want to do the same.

I am so thankful that God is pouring out His Holy Spirit on all flesh. Young men and young women are prophesying. Young men are seeing visions, and old men are dreaming dreams. The Holy Spirit is my Helper and my Comforter. I love Him.

The Holy Spirit is empowering me to be a witness for my Savior, Jesus Christ. Praise His name! His presence in my life enables me to speak the Word of God with boldness. The Holy Spirit always testifies of Jesus.

God is helping me to walk in the fear of the Lord and the comfort of the Holy Spirit. I now know that the Kingdom of God does not consist of eating and drinking, but of righteousness, peace, and joy in the Holy Spirit.

The grace of the Lord Jesus Christ, the love of God, and the communion of the Holy Spirit are mine forever! Hallelujah!

Related Scriptures: 1 Corinthians 6:19; John 14:16-17; Ephesians 5:18; John 16:13-15; John 16:7; Joel 2:28; Acts 1:8; Acts 4:31; John 15:26; Acts 9:31; Romans 15:17; 2 Corinthians 13:14.

Personal Prayer: Heavenly Father, I thank you for the Holy Spirit. He reminds me that if I ask anything in the name of Jesus Christ, you will do it for me. What a blessed truth this is. I love you, your Son, Jesus, and the Holy Spirit who resides within me. I want to keep all your commandments, and I know the Holy Spirit will help me to do so. The Holy Spirit is my constant companion and my Comforter, and I know He will abide with me forever. In Jesus' name I pray, Amen.

A Promise to Claim: "But after that the kindness and love of God our Saviour toward man appeared, not by works of righteousness which we have done, but according to his mercy he saved us, by the washing of regeneration, and renewing of the Holy Ghost; which he shed on us abundantly through Jesus Christ our Saviour; that being justified by his grace, we should be made heirs according to the hope of eternal life" (Titus 3:4-7).

Words of Wisdom: *"We must be, we must be, we must be baptized with the Holy Spirit—and refilled time and again as our service for God necessitates it"* (R.A. Torrey).

Hope

Affirmation of Fatih: Hope is the anchor of my soul. My hope is in the Lord who made Heaven and Earth.

The Lord is my portion, saith my soul; therefore will I hope in him.

(LAMENTATIONS 3:22-24)

Central Focus: Our God is the God of all hope. The hope He imparts to us gives us joy and peace. He is our hope, so there is no room for hopelessness. His hope lifts you above life's circumstances.

Meditation on God's Promises to You: The God of all hope is filling me with all joy and peace in believing, that I will be able to abound in hope through the power of the Holy Ghost. I rejoice in the hope He gives to me, because I know His hope will never let me be ashamed. The love of God is shed abroad in my heart by the Holy Spirit. Hallelujah!

The hope of salvation is my helmet, and this protects my mind. His mercy is upon me, as I hope in Him. God is my hiding place and my shield. I completely hope in His Word. I do my work in hope so that I know I will be a partaker of His hope.

I lay hold upon the hope that is set before me. This blessed hope is an anchor for my soul. It is both sure and steadfast. I am so thankful for the hope God has imparted to me. During these times of evil, God is my hope.

I glory in tribulations because I know that tribulation works patience, patience works experience, and experience works hope. God is giving me the spirit of wisdom and revelation in the knowledge of Him. The eyes of my understanding are being enlightened, that I might know the hope of His calling and what the riches of the glory of His inheritance in the saints are.

He is revealing to me the exceeding greatness of His power, as I learn to believe in Him, according to His mighty power, which He wrought in Christ when He raised Him from the dead. He has set Him at His own right hand in the heavenly places, far above all principality, power, might, dominion, and every name that is named, not only in this world, but also in that which is to come. This knowledge gives me great hope indeed.

God is showing me the riches of the glory of the mystery which was hidden for ages, and this mystery is Christ in me, the hope of glory. Yes, Jesus lives within me and this gives me great hope. My hope, joy, and crown of rejoicing are related to the presence of Jesus Christ at His coming.

In light of His goodness to me, I will live soberly, righteously, and godly in this present world. I will look for the blessed hope, which is the glorious appearing of my great God and the Lord Jesus Christ, who gave himself for me, that He might redeem me from iniquity and purify me.

Related Scriptures: Romans 15:13; Romans 5:1-5; 1 Thessalonians 5:8; Psalm 33:22; 1 Corinthians 9:10; Jeremiah 17:17; Romans 5:4; Ephesians 1:17-21; Colossians 1:26-28; Titus 2:13-14.

Personal Prayer: I put all my hope in you, Father. Thank you for the gift of hope that enables me to look forward to the future with great joy and anticipation. You are the God of all hope, and I will walk with you. As I do so, I know you will fill my heart with hope and faith that are based upon your promises that prevail. You are my hope, dear Lord. In Jesus' name I pray, Amen.

A Promise to Claim: "Blessed be the God and Father of our Lord Jesus Christ, which according to his abundant mercy hath begotten us again unto a lively hope by the resurrection of Jesus Christ from the dead, to an inheritance incorruptible, and undefiled, and that fadeth not away, reserved in heaven for you, who are kept by the power of God through faith unto salvation ready to be revealed in the last time" (1 Peter 1:3-5).

Words of Wisdom: *"Holding the Word of God in your heart until it has affected every phase of your life—this is meditation"* (Andrew Murray).

26

Humility

Affirmation of Faith: Humility is the opposite of pride, and pride is a deadly sin. God is clothing me with humility that keeps me from ever entering the realm of pride.

> *The fear of the Lord is the instruction of wisdom; and before honour is humility.*

(PROVERBS 15:33)

Central Focus: As we learn to humble ourselves under God's almighty hand, He will enable us to resist the devil, who will flee from us. Humility leads to honor and victory. Humility always comes before honor, but pride always goes before a fall. Determine in your heart to walk in humility

Meditation on God's Promises to You: Riches, honor and life come to me through humility and the fear of the Lord. I humble myself before the Lord and pray and seek His face. As I do so, I know He will hear from Heaven and forgive me. Praise the Lord for this blessed promise.

I know that God never forgets the cry of a humble person. The Lord is my King forever, and He hears my desire as I humble myself and He prepares my heart and causes my ears to hear. Hallelujah! I will bless Him at all times, and His praise shall continually be in my mouth. My soul will make its boast in Him, and the humble will hear me and be glad.

Pride goes before destruction and a haughty spirit before a fall. Therefore, I know it is better to be of a humble spirit with the lowly than to divide the spoil with the proud. While a man's pride will bring him low, honor will uphold the humble in spirit. I choose to remain humble in spirit.

It amazes me to know that the high and lofty One who inhabits eternity dwells with me when my spirit is humble and contrite. He revives my spirit. I, therefore, humble myself as a child, because I know that child-like faith is needed for entrance into the Kingdom of Heaven.

God's Word promises me that those who exalt themselves will be abased and those who humble themselves will be exalted. God gives His grace to me, and He keeps on giving. Therefore, I submit to Him, and, as I resist the devil, I know Satan will flee from me. As I draw near to God, I know He draws near to me. Therefore, I cleanse my hands and purify my heart. I humble myself in the Lord's sight, and, as I do so, He lifts me up.

From this point on I will serve the Lord with all humility of mind. I choose to be clothed with humility, for I know that God resists the proud and gives grace to the humble. I need His grace; therefore, I humble myself under His almighty hand, knowing that He will exalt me.

Related Scriptures: Proverbs 22:4; 2 Chronicles 7:14; Psalm 9:12; Proverbs 10:16-17; Psalm 34:1-2; Proverbs 16:19; Proverbs 29:23; Isaiah 57:15; Matthew 18:3-4; Matthew 23:12; James 4:6-10; 1 Peter 5:5-10.

Personal Prayer: Heavenly Father, it is not easy to be humble, but I know this is what you want from me. Help me to esteem others as being better than myself and to walk in lowliness of mind. Help me never to think more highly of myself than I ought to think. Thank you for the honor you promise to me if I learn to walk in humility. Fearing you, dear God, I know you will clothe me with your humility. In Jesus' name I pray, Amen.

A Promise to Claim: "Before destruction the heart of man is haughty, and before honour is humility" (Proverbs 18:12).

Words of Wisdom: *"True humility is not thinking less of yourself; it is thinking of yourself less"* (C.S. Lewis).

27

Inheritance

Affirmation of Faith: The gifts of God are already mine. He had made me a joint-heir with Jesus.

> *Blessed be the God and Father of our Lord*
> *Jesus Christ, Who hath blessed*
> *us with all spiritual blessings in heavenly*
> *places in Christ.*

(EPHESIANS 1:3)

Central Focus: God has adopted us into His family, and this means we are now joint-heirs with His precious Son, Jesus. He has given us an incorruptible inheritance that makes us rich indeed. As God's child, you are an inheritor of all His blessings. Never minimize or discount this truth, for He has already granted your inheritance to you.

Meditation on God's Promises to You: I am so blessed to be a child of God who enjoys the wonderful inheritance He has promised to His children. I have obtained that blessed inheritance already, because I was predestined to receive it according to His purpose. I am so thankful that He works all things after the counsel of His own will.

My Father has given me so many wonderful things through Christ. I am enjoying His inheritance, and I am deeply grateful for all He has given to me. I am so thankful for the Word of His grace, which builds me up and gives me an inheritance among all those who are sanctified.

It thrills me to know that Abba-Father has adopted me into His family. As one of His children, I am an heir of God, a joint-heir with Jesus Christ. I was chosen in Him, having been predestinated according to His plan. I thank Him for working everything out according to the purpose of His will. I will ever live for the praise of His glory.

Because I believed, I was marked in Him with a seal, the promised Holy Spirit. I am so thankful for the Holy Spirit. He guarantees my inheritance. Hallelujah! God has justified me according to His grace, and this enables me to be an heir who has the hope of eternal life. I will diligently hearken unto His voice and be obedient to His teachings.

It blesses my heart to know that God promises so many blessings to me. His blessings are truly overtaking me. I know I will be blessed in the city and blessed in the field. I know that the fruit of my body shall be blessed and so will be the fruit of my ground. My basket and my store shall be blessed as well. I am blessed as I come in and as I go out. I claim these blessings for my life right now.

God has shown me that my inheritance includes the fact that my enemies will be smitten. He is commanding His blessing on my storehouses and everything that I set my hand to do. This truly is a wonderful inheritance. I am so thankful for all the blessings of His inheritance that I am already enjoying as His child. Praise His holy name!

Related Scriptures: Ephesians 1:11; Acts 20:32; Romans 8:16; Ephesians 1:11; Titus 3:7; Deuteronomy 28.

Personal Prayer: Abba-Father, I thank you for adopting me into your family. As a result, I have so many blessings on a daily basis. In fact, you daily load me with benefits for which I am so grateful. In the inheritance you've given to me, I find everything I need for godly living. Thank you for your forgiveness, love, joy, faith, hope, and all the abundant blessings you've given to me. I am blessed indeed. In Jesus' name I pray, Amen.

A Promise to Claim: "In whom ye also trusted, after that ye heard the word of truth, the gospel of your salvation: in whom also after that ye believed, ye were sealed with that holy spirit of promise, which is the earnest of our inheritance until the redemption of the purchased possession, unto the praise of his glory" (Ephesians 1:13-14).

Words of Wisdom: *"The unthankful heart discovers no mercies; but the thankful heart will find, in every hour, some heavenly blessings"* (Henry Ward Beecher).

28

Intercession

Affirmation of Faith: I will pray for others in the same way that Jesus and the Holy Spirit are praying for me.

> *Praying always with all prayer and supplication in the Spirit, and watching thereunto with all perseverance and supplication for all saints; And I say unto you, Ask, and it shall be given you; seek, and ye shall find; knock, and it shall be opened unto you.*

(EPHESIANS 6:18)

Central Focus: Jesus ever lives to make intercession for us. Strive to be like Him in every respect—compassionate, caring, and filled with love for others. It is these qualities that will lead you to be an intercessor. Intercession is a vitally important ministry that every believer can engage in at any time. Pray for others as you pray for yourself.

Meditation on God's Promises to You: The Lord Jesus Christ is my High Priest, and He is praying for me now. I know He cares and that He knows what I am going through. My weakness is His opportunity to prove His strength. I can do all things through Him.

How thankful I am that He truly understands me. He knows what I need. The Lord Jesus is the mediator between me and God, the Father, and He always lives to make intercession for me. Jesus knows the power of prayer. It was through prayer that He learned His Father's will, and through prayer I will do the same. Jesus gained strength to overcome temptation through prayer, as well. He developed a deeply intimate, personal relationship with His Father, and I want to do the same. Jesus taught me how to pray, and He stressed its importance for my life.

No temptation has come to me but such as is common to all. God is able to deliver me from all temptations and from the evil one. I am so thankful that Jesus and the angels are fighting on my behalf. My Lord has already won the battle. Tempted in all points as I have been, He never sinned. Now that He lives within me and continues to intercede on my behalf, the power of the Holy Spirit will help me win all my personal battles.

Jesus prayed that God would supply my daily bread, and He always has. He prayed that God's Kingdom would come to Earth, and now the King resides within me. In fact, the Kingdom of God is within me. I realize that His wonderful Kingdom does not consist of meat and drink, but it is righteousness, peace, and joy in the Holy Spirit.

I owe so much to the intercession of Jesus, and I have learned so much about this important activity from Him. Therefore, I will faithfully intercede for my family, friends, ministries, church leaders, and other needs that I become aware of.

Related Scriptures: Hebrews 9:11; Hebrews 7:25; Hebrews 4:15; 2 Corinthians 12:9; Philippians 4:13; Psalm 139:23-24; Matthew 6:8; 1 Timothy 2:5; Hebrews 7:25; Luke 6:12; Mark 14:36; Luke 22:29-46; John 17; Luke 11:1-13; Matthew 21:13; 1 Corinthians 10:13; Luke 11:4; John 19:30; Hebrews 4:15; Luke 11:1-13; Matthew 21:13; Colossians 1:27; Romans 14:17.

Personal Prayer: Heavenly Father, I come to you in the full knowledge that Jesus truly cares. He has made it possible for me to have direct access to you. He had atoned for all my sins. The Lord Jesus Christ is the way, the truth, and the life, and this knowledge assures me that you hear me when I pray and that you will undertake to answer my prayers. Thank you, Lord. I also know that you hear your Son and the Holy Spirit as they intercede for me. Glory to you! In the name of Jesus I pray, Amen.

A Promise to Claim: "Casting all your care upon him; for he careth for you" (1 Peter 5:7).

Words of Wisdom: *"Prayer is not a discourse. It is a form of life, the life with God. That is why it is not confined to the moment of verbal statement"* (Jacques Ellul).

29

Jesus

Affirmation of Faith: Jesus is the King of kings and the Lord of lords. He is my personal Savior and Lord.

> *But we see Jesus, who was made a little lower than the angels for the suffering of death,*
> *crowned with glory and honour; that he by the grace of God should taste death for every man.*

(HEBREWS 2:9)

Central Focus: Jesus is the center of human history, and He should be the center of your life. He is your Savior, Lord, and soon-coming King. The name of Jesus is so sweet. It is like the fragrance of spring flowers. Keep your focus on Him, for He is the Author and Finisher of your faith.

Meditation on God's Promises to You: My spirit rejoices in God my Savior. He came to seek and to save that which is lost.

Jesus is my Lord. It is good for me to draw near to Him. I have put my total trust in Him, and I will declare all His works. I will let Him dwell in my heart by faith, that I, being rooted and grounded in love, may be able to comprehend with all the saints what is the breadth, and length, and depth, and height of God's love. I want to know the love of Christ, which passes knowledge, that I might be filled with all the fullness of God.

Jesus is my peace. He has made both one and has broken down the middle wall of partition between us. I will be anxious about nothing, but in everything by prayer and supplication with thanksgiving I will let my requests be made known unto God. As I do so, I know the peace of God, which surpasses all understanding, shall keep your hearts and minds through Jesus Christ.

Jesus is my forgiveness. Jesus is my advocate with the Father. He is the righteous one. As far as the East is from the West, so far has He removed our transgressions from us.

Jesus is my righteousness. He is made unto me wisdom, righteousness, and sanctification. He lives within me. Therefore, my body is dead because of sin, but the Spirit is life because of righteousness.

Jesus is my Deliverer. The law of the Spirit of life in Christ Jesus has made me free from the law of sin and death. He has given me the power to tread upon serpents and scorpions and over all the power of the enemy. Therefore, I know that nothing shall be able to hurt me.

Jesus is my example. Christ suffered for me, thereby leaving me an example, that I should follow His steps. I will abide in Him, and I will walk as He walked.

Jesus is my constant companion. He will never leave me nor forsake me. He will never leave me comfortless.

Jesus is my Brother. I want to do the will of God at all times, for as I do so, I will experience brotherhood with Jesus Christ. I have received Him, and He has given me power to become a child of God, because I believe upon His holy name.

Jesus is my guardian. He is a shield for me, my glory, and the lifter of my head. He leads me, and I am His child. He is so faithful to me. He will establish me and keep me from all evil. Hallelujah!

Jesus is my security. Nothing shall ever be able to separate me from the love of God, which is in Jesus Christ my Lord. Surely goodness and mercy shall follow me all the days of my life, and I will dwell in the house of the Lord forever.

Jesus is my sufficiency. He is all that I need. I can do all things through Him, for He strengthens me. I abide in Him and His words abide in me. Therefore, I will ask what I will, and I know it shall be done unto me.

Jesus is everything to me. He supplies all my need according to His riches in glory. Whatever I ask, I receive of Him, because I keep His commandments and always endeavor to do those things that are pleasing in His sight.

Related Scriptures: Luke 1:47; Luke 19;10; Psalm 73:28; Ephesians 3:17-19; Ephesians 2:a4; Philippians 4:6-7; 1 John 2:1; Psalm 203:12; 1 Corinthians 1:30; Romans 8:10; Romans 8:2; Luke 10:19; 1 Peter 2:21; 1 John 2:6; Hebrews 13:5; John 14:8; Matthew 12:50; 1 John 1:12; Psalm 3:3; Romans 8:14; 2 Thessalonians 3:3; Romans 8:39; Psalm 23:6; Philippians 4:13; John 15:7; Philippians 4:19.

Personal Prayer: Lord God, I thank you for sending Jesus to be my Savior and Lord. He is everything to me. I love Him because He first loved me and gave himself for me. How I praise you, Father, that you have given me the victory through Jesus Christ, my Lord. Because He lives, I can face tomorrow. Because He lives, all fear is gone. Death no longer has a sting and the grave no longer has any victory. Because He lives, I can live the abundant, eternal life He has given to me. Because He lives, I have been set free. In His precious name I pray, Amen.

A Promise to Claim: "And ye are complete in him, which is the head of all principality and power" (Colossians 2:10).

Words of Wisdom: *Jesus knows everything about you, yet He loves you with His everlasting love.*

30

Light

Affirmation of Faith: "This little light of mine—I'm going to let it shine." Jesus is the Light of my life and the light of the world.

That was the true Light, which lighteth every man that cometh into the world.

(JOHN 1:9)

Central Focus: Jesus is the light of the world. His light overwhelms all darkness. Let the light of Jesus shine through you wherever you go. In so doing, you will always dispel the darkness of this world.

Meditation on God's Promises to You: The Lord is my light. I will walk in the light as He is in the light. His Word is a lamp unto my feet and a light unto my path. I will walk in the light it sheds each step of my way. The Lord truly is the light of my life.

I trust in Him with all my heart, not leaning upon my own understanding. In all my ways I will acknowledge Him, and I know He will direct my steps. Because His is my light and my salvation, I will not fear anyone or anything. Though a host of people or other forces encamp against me, I will not fear. God's love and light give me great confidence and strength.

I will dwell in the house of the Lord all the days of my life, and I will dwell there forever, knowing that goodness and mercy will always follow me. My heavenly Father lifts the light of His countenance upon me and gives me His peace.

He has put gladness in my heart. In Him there is a fountain of life, and in His light I see light. He has taken me out of the kingdom of darkness and has placed me in His marvelous kingdom of light. He will light my candle in the darkness. The entrance of His words brings light to my spirit.

He is light, and in Him there is no darkness at all. He cleanses me from all sin—past, present, and future—and this enables me to walk in the light as He is in the light.

Related Scriptures: Psalm 27:1; 1 John 1:7; Psalm 119:105; 1 John 1:9; Proverbs 3:5-6; Psalm 27:1; Psalm 27:3; Psalm 23:6; Psalm 4:6; Psalm 4:7; Psalm 36:9; 1 Peter 2:9; Psalm 18:28; Psalm 119:130; 1 John 1:5; 1 John 1:6.

Personal Prayer: Father, enlighten the eyes of my understanding so that I will know the hope of your calling and what the riches of the glory of your inheritance are in the saints. Let your light shine through so that I will know your exceeding power in my life through faith in your promises. Let your mighty power work in and through me. I want to be a light to the world in the same way that Jesus is the Light of the world. In His name I pray, Amen.

A Promise to Claim: "The Lord is my light and my salvation; whom shall I fear? The Lord is the strength of my life; of whom shall I be afraid?" (Psalm 27:1).

Words of Wisdom: *"If we walk in the light, as he is in the light, we have fellowship with one another, and the blood of Jesus Christ his son cleanseth us from all sin"* (I John 1:7).

Love

Affirmation of Faith: God's love casts out all fear. His love is unconditional and never-ending. I love Him, because He first loved me.

> *But God commendeth his love toward us, in*
> *that, while we were yet sinners,*
> *Christ died for us.*

(ROMANS 5:8)

Central Focus: God is love, and His love compels us to walk in love at all times. Let love be without hypocrisy in your life. (See Romans 12:9.) Love one another, and remember he that loves knows God, because God is love.

Meditation on God's Promises to You: God so loved the world that He gave His only begotten Son, that whosoever believes in Him should not perish but have everlasting life. Therefore, it behooves us to love one another, for everyone who loves knows God, but he who does not love does not know God.

No one has seen God at any time. If we love one another, however, God dwells within us and His love is perfected in us. I want Christ to always dwell within my heart by faith, and I want to be rooted and grounded in His love, that I may be able to comprehend with all saints what is the breadth, length, depth, and height of God's love. In this way I will know the love of Christ, which surpasses knowledge, that I might be filled with all God's fullness.

How thankful I am that God's love for me is everlasting and that He has drawn me to himself with His kindness. I will obey Jesus' command to love others. I love the Lord, and I will seek Him early each day, realizing that He loves those who love Him.

It is my heart's desire to keep all God's command-ments that are declared in His Word. As I do so, I know I will experience His love and I know He will manifest himself to me. The Lord will command His loving-kindness in the daytime, and in the night His song shall be with me. Because of this, I will pray unto Him, for He is the God of my life.

And now abides faith, hope, and love—these three, but the greatest of these is love. I am persuaded that neither death, life, angels, principalities, powers, things present, things to come, height, depth, nor any other creature shall be able to separate me from the love of God, which is in Christ Jesus my Lord.

I will walk in love from this time forth, and I will speak the truth in love. Likewise, I will receive others as Christ has received me and bear the fruit of love in all my relationships and responsibilities. I will let my faith be expressed through love, as I love the Lord God with all my heart, soul, and strength and love my neighbor as myself.

Related Scriptures: John 3:16; 1 John 4:7-12; Ephesians 3:17-19; Jeremiah 31:3; John 15:17; Proverbs 8:17; John 14:21; Psalm 42:8; 1 Corinthians 13:13; Romans 8:38-39; 1 John 2:6; Ephesians 4:15; Romans 15:7; Galatians 5:22; Galatians 5:6; Matthew 22:37; Matthew 22:39.

Personal Prayer: Dear God, my Father, I love you with all my heart, soul, mind, and strength. I praise you for commending your love toward me in that while I was yet a sinner, Christ died for me. This is true love. I thank you that you are loved personified. Continuously fill me with the Holy Spirit, Lord, so that I will be able to produce the fruit of your love in all the relationships and responsibilities of my life. I praise you that your banner over me is always LOVE. In the loving name of Jesus I pray, Amen.

A Promise to Claim: "Greater love has no one that this, that he lay down his life for his friends" (John 15:12-13).

Words of Wisdom: *"God is clearly deserving of our love especially if we consider who He is that loves us, who we are that He loves, and how much He loves us"* (Bernard of Clairvaux).

Meditation

Affirmation of Faith: Through Bible meditation I am able to receive all God's promises, and I know that His promises always prevail. I receive and believe His promises.

> Eye has not seen, nor ear heard, nor have
>   entered into the heart of man the
> things which God has prepared for those
>   who love Him—but God has revealed
>   them to us
> through His Spirit.

(1 CORINTHIANS 2:9-10, NKJV)

Central Focus: Meditation upon God's Word changes your mindset and enables you to see things from God's perspective. God is watching over you, and all His special promises are yours! In the same way that a cow chews its cud, the believer chews on (ruminates upon) God's Word, letting its truths soak into his innermost being and filling his spiritual hunger.

Meditation on God's Promises to You: God's Word will not depart from my mouth. I will meditate upon it day and night so that I may observe to do according to all that is written therein. It is then that my way will be prosperous and I shall have good success. It gives me great happiness to know that as I walk not in the counsel of the ungodly nor stand in the path of sinners nor sit in the seat of the scornful, I will find my delight in God's Word [and His promises] and I will meditate both day and night upon His Word. Therefore, I shall become like a tree planted by the rivers of water, that brings forth its fruit in its season, and my leaf shall not wither. Whatever I do shall prosper. Hallelujah!

God is a promise-keeper and He wants me to be a promise-reaper. He is the giver of every good and perfect gift, the Father of lights with whom there is no variableness nor shadow of turning. He is ready to perform His Word on my behalf.

Heaven and Earth will pass away, but God's Word will never pass away. The Father has magnified His Word above His name. I believe the words that were written by the Prophet Isaiah: "For as the rain comes down. . . . So shall My word be that goes forth from My mouth; it shall not return to Me void, but it shall accomplish what I please, and it shall prosper in the thing for which I sent it" (Isaiah 55:10-11, NKJV).

God always hastens His Word to perform it. Meditation upon God's Word is one of life's greatest experiences.

Related Scriptures: Joshua 1:8; Psalm 1:1-3; James 1:16-17; Jeremiah 1:12; Matthew 24:35; Psalm 138:2; Isaiah 55:10-11; Jeremiah 1:12

Personal Prayer: Heavenly Father, I love to meditate upon your Word. It a treasure chest that is filled with precious gems and gold nuggets. Your Word is a lamp unto my feet and a light unto my path. As I meditate upon your Word, I am strengthened and made happy. The power of your Word flows into my spirit and enables me to prevail in every challenge and circumstance I faith. Thank you for your Word of truth, Father. I will hide it in my heart so as not to sin against you. In Jesus' name I pray, Amen.

A Promise to Claim: "O how I love thy law! It is my meditation all the day. Thou through thy commandments hast made me wiser than mine enemies: for they are ever with me" (Psalm 119:97-98).

Words of Wisdom: *Take time to meditate upon God's Word every day. This will truly change your mind, your attitude, and your perspective.*

33

Mercy

Affirmation of faith: I want to always extend mercy to others in the same way that God has extended His mercy to me. I will let His mercy always triumph over judgment in my life and in my dealings with others.

> *Hear me when I call, O God of my*
> *righteousness; thou hast enlarged*
> *me when*
> *I was in distress; have mercy upon me,*
> *and hear my prayer.*

(PSALM 4:1)

Central Focus: God's mercy is freely available to us. His mercy involves kindness, compassion, and love. With His help I will become a merciful person. Surely goodness and mercy shall follow me all the days of my life, and I will dwell in the house of the Lord forever.

Meditation on God's Promises to You: The Father is helping me to walk in mercy. I need His help, and I trust in His mercy as my heart rejoices in His salvation. I will sing unto the Lord, for He has always dealt bountifully with me. Surely goodness and mercy will follow me all the days of my life, and I will dwell in the Lord's house forever. Praise His holy name!

He is showing me His ways and teaching me His paths. He is leading me in His truth and teaching me, for He is the God of my salvation. I wait on Him all day long. His tender mercies and loving-kindnesses have been ever of old.

I will be glad and rejoice in His mercy, for I know He has always considered my troubles and has known my soul in the midst of troubles. His eyes are upon me, as I hope in His mercy. He is my defense. He is the God of mercy, and I will ever sing unto Him. He is ever the God of my mercy and my defense. I thank God that He is reviving me that I would ever rejoice in Him.

Daily He is showing me His mercy. It blesses me to know that mercy and truth have met together and righteousness and peace have kissed each other. As He continues to teach me His way, I will walk in His truth. As He unites my heart to fear His name, I will praise Him with all my heart and I will glorify His name forevermore.

I am so thankful for His great mercy and compassion. God is gracious, longsuffering, and plenteous in mercy and truth. Therefore, I come into His presence with singing. He is the God who has made me, and I am a sheep in His pasture. I enter His gates with thanksgiving and go into His courts with praise. I am so thankful to Him, and I bless His holy name.

Related Scriptures: Psalm 6; Psalm 13; Psalm 23; Psalm 25; Psalm 31; Psalm 33; Psalm 59; Psalm 85; Psalm 86; Psalm 100.

Personal Prayer: Father, your mercy is from everlasting to everlasting. I want to be merciful to others in the same way you have been merciful to me. Thank you for your great mercy, Lord. I believe your promise which says, "Blessed are the merciful: for they shall obtain mercy." Help me to walk in mercy toward others at all times, Father. In Jesus' name, Amen.

A Promise to Claim: "Blessed be the God and Father of our Lord Jesus Christ, which according to His abundant mercy hath begotten us again unto a lively hope by the resurrection of Jesus Christ from the dead" (1 Peter 1:3).

Words of Wisdom: *"The Lord's goodness surrounds us at every moment. I walk through it almost with difficulty, as through thick grass and flowers"* (R.W. Barbour).

34

Might (Power)

Affirmation of Faith: Almighty God is all-powerful. He can do anything, and He is with me each day. He also lives within me, and all His power and might are available to me.

> *That he would grant you, according to the*
> *riches of his glory,*
> *to be strengthened with might by his Spirit*
> *in the inner man; that Christ*
> *may dwell in your hearts by faith.*

(EPHESIANS 3:16-17)

Central Focus: All power within Heaven and Earth resides in you, because Jesus lives in you. To gain God's might and power, you must be weak in your own strength. Remember, His strength is made perfect in weakness.

Meditation on God's Promises to You: God is strengthening me by His Word, as I meditate upon His truths. In quietness and in confidence shall be my strength. Through His grace I will walk worthy of

Him unto all pleasing, and I shall be fruitful in every good work as I increase in my knowledge of Him.

He is strengthening me with all might, according to His glorious power, unto all patience and longsuffering with joyfulness. Therefore, I give thanks unto the Father who has made me meet to be a partaker of the inheritance of the saints in light.

I will wait upon the Lord, and I shall renew my strength. I will mount up with wings as an eagle. I shall run and not be weary. I shall walk and not faint. The joy of the Lord is my strength. I can do all things through Christ who strengthens me. Indeed, He is my strength.

There is never a reason for fear, for the Lord is with me. I will not be dismayed, for He is my God. He is strengthening me and helping me. He is upholding me with His right hand of righteousness. He gives power to the faint, and He increases my strength.

The Lord is my rock and my fortress. He is my Deliverer and my God. He is my strength, and I will ever trust in Him. He is my buckler and the horn of my salvation. He is my high tower. Hallelujah! I put on the whole armor of God that I may be able to stand in the evil day and having done all, to stand firmly.

The Lord is my light and my salvation. Whom shall I fear? The Lord is the strength of my life. Of whom shall I be afraid? Therefore, I will be strong in the Lord and in the power of His might.

Related Scriptures: Psalm 119:28; Isaiah 30:15; Colossians 1:10-12; Isaiah 40:31; Nehemiah 8:10; Philippians 4:13; Isaiah 41:10; Isaiah 40:29; Psalm 18:2; Ephesians 6:13; Psalm 27:1; Ephesians 6:10.

Personal Prayer: My loving Father, you are my strength. I will always love you. Thank you so much for strengthening, empowering, and helping me in all the situations of my life. I will walk in your strength, knowing that you are my rock and my fortress. Yes, Lord, you are my God, my strength, my buckler, the horn of my salvation, and my high tower. You have made me strong. In Jesus' name I pray, Amen.

A Promise to Claim: "Now unto him that is able to do exceeding abundantly above all that we ask or think, according to the power that worketh in us, unto him be glory in the church by Christ Jesus throughout all ages, world without end. Amen" (Ephesians 3:20-21).

Words of Wisdom: *"When we cultivate the inner person through prayer, meditation on the Word, and submission to the Lord, then we can experience the joys of a disciplined and diligent life"* (Warren Wiersbe).

Mourning (Grief)

Affirmation of Faith: Grief and mourning become my experience every time I lose someone or something that is important to me, but I will always remember that God is going through the grief and mourning with me. He cares, and I will never lose Him.

Yes, though I walk through the valley of the shadow of death, I will fear no evil: for thou art with me.

(PSALM 23:4)

Central Focus: The love of God will sustain you, no matter what you are going through. He loves you with an everlasting love. Earth has no sorrow that Heaven cannot heal.

Meditation on God's Promises to You: The Lord God is my helper. He is turning my mourning into dancing. He has put off my sackcloth and girded me with gladness to the end that my glory may sing praise to Him and not be silent. I will give thanks to Him forever. Hallelujah!

With joy I shall return and come with singing unto Zion. Everlasting joy will be upon my head, and I will obtain gladness and joy. When that happens, I know that all sorrow and mourning shall flee from me. God is my everlasting light and my glory. He has promised to me that the days of mourning and grief will end.

The Father has poured out His Spirit upon me, and He has anointed me to preach good tidings to the meek, to bind up the broken-hearted, to proclaim liberty to the captives, and the opening of prison to all who are bound. He wants me to proclaim the acceptable year of the Lord and the day of vengeance of our God. This I will do, as I reach out with His comfort to all those who mourn.

Abba-Father is giving me beauty for ashes. Praise His name. He is giving me the oil of joy for mourning and the garment of praise for the spirit of heaviness, that I might be called a tree of righteousness, the planting of the Lord. Thereby He shall be glorified in and through my life. He is helping me to become a watered garden so that I will not sorrow anymore. As a result, I shall be able to rejoice in spite of all sorrow and loss.

Though there is a time to weep and to mourn, God is helping me to rise up from my grief and mourning so that I will ever praise Him. His wonderful promise of comfort helps me to know that I am blessed even in this time of mourning.

Related Scriptures: Psalm 30:10-12; Isaiah 51:11; Isaiah 60:19-20; Isaiah 61:1-2; Isaiah 61:3; Jeremiah 31:13; Ecclesiastes 3:4; Matthew 5:4.

Personal Prayer: Heavenly Father, thank you for always being there for me even in times of grief and mourning. Even when I have to walk through the shadow of death, I know you are with me and you are comforting me. You are the God of all comfort, and I receive comfort from you as I stand upon your promises and spend time alone with you. I love you, Lord. In Jesus' name I pray, Amen.

A Promise to Claim: "Surely goodness and mercy shall follow me all the days of my life: and I will dwell in the house of the Lord forever" (Psalm 23:6).

Words of Wisdom: *"But death is given no power over love. Love is stronger. It creates something new out of the destruction caused by death; it bears everything and overcomes everything"* (Paul Tillich).

Negativity

Affirmation of Faith: I will let go of all negativity, resentment, bitterness, and hatred. These things have the power to defile myself and others. (See Hebrews 12:15.)

> *Finally, brethren, whatsoever things are true, whatsoever things are honest, whatsoever things are just,*
> *whatsoever things are pure, whatsoever things are lovely, whatsoever things are of good report;*
> *if there be any praise, think on these things.*

(PHILIPPIANS 4:8)

Central Focus: We need to become yes-yes believers in a no-no world. Jesus is our role-model, our Savior, and our Lord. His positive approach to things is a positive example for us to follow at all times. As Christians, we must always remain positive in our thinking, our outlook, and especially in our words. Negativity in any form should not have a place in our lives.

Meditation on God's Promises to You: I resist any attempt for my mind to go in negative directions, and I will focus on those things that are honest, just, pure, lovely, and of good report. This changes my perspective about everything. The Lord God is the portion of my inheritance and my lot. Therefore, I have a goodly inheritance. I really appreciate His counsel from His Word, and I will make every effort to apply it to my life. His prevailing promises shall sustain me.

I have set the Lord before me. Because He is at my right hand, I know I shall not be moved. My heart is glad and my glory rejoices. My flesh shall rest in hope. I am so thankful that God has shown me the path of life. In His presence there is fullness of joy, and at His right hand there are pleasures forevermore. Knowing these truths, I rise above all negativity and choose a positive perspective and approach regarding everything in my life and all circumstances around me.

The Lord is my light and my salvation. Therefore, I have nothing to fear. He is the strength of my life. Therefore, I will never be afraid of anyone. I extol the Lord, for He has lifted me up, and I know my foes will not rejoice over me. As I cry unto the Lord, He heals me. Hallelujah!

I will bless the Lord at all times. His praise shall continually be in my mouth. My soul will make its boast in Him. The humble shall hear about this and be glad. I seek the Lord, and I know He hears me and delivers me from all my fears and from all negativity.

According to His multitude of loving-kindnesses, God has mercy upon me. His tender mercies blot out all of my transgressions. He washes me thoroughly from my iniquity and He cleanses me from my sins. Hallelujah!

God is leading me in positive, new directions. Hallelujah!

Related Scriptures: Philippians 4:8; Psalm 16:5-9; Psalm 16:11; Psalm 27:1; Psalm 30:1-2; Psalm 34:1-4; Psalm 51:1-4.

Personal Prayer: Dear Lord, thank you for reminding me to be positive at all times. I know that negative thoughts and words are harmful to my soul. Through your grace I rise above all negativity and I purpose in my heart to serve you in proactive, positive ways at all times. I will seek first your kingdom and your righteousness, and I know that as I do so, I will see many positive results. Help me to keep my heart positive with all diligence, and may the words of my mouth encourage others. In Jesus' name I pray, Amen.

A Promise to Claim: "If you keep My commandments, you will abide in My love, just as I have kept My Father's commandments and abide in His love. These thing I have spoken to you, that My joy may remain in you, and that your joy may be full" (John 15:10-11, NKJV).

Words of Wisdom: *"Kind words produce their images on men's souls"* (Blaise Pascal).

Patience

Affirmation of Faith: Waiting requires patience and endurance, and God wants me to wait upon Him and to wait for the fulfillment of His promises in my life.

> *Wait on the Lord; be of good courage, and He shall strengthen your heart; wait, I say, on the Lord!"*

(PSALM 27:14, NKJV)

Central Focus: It is through faith and patience that we inherit all God's promises. (See Hebrews 6:12.) To be patient, we must learn to endure hardships and difficulties through God's grace. Remember, it is His grace that enables you to do so.

Meditation on God's Promises to You: One fruit of God's indwelling Spirit is patience (longsuffering). He is developing this fruit in my life as I learn to put Him first at all times. I will wait upon the Lord, and, as I do so, He renews my strength. I will mount up with wings as eagles. I will run and not be weary. I will walk and not faint. Praise God for His strength in my life.

I choose to wait upon the Lord and be of good courage. He will strengthen my heart, as I learn to wait on Him. As I hope for what I do not see, patience grows within me.

I rest in the Lord and wait patiently for Him. I will not be fretful or slothful. Instead, I will be a follower of them, who through faith and patience inherit the promises. I will be one of them!

I will not cast my confidence away. I know I have need of patience, that, after I have done the will of God, I will receive His promise. I believe that the Lord's return is imminent, and I will patiently await His arrival.

As I let patience develop within me, I lay aside every weight and the sin which easily besets me, and I run with patience the race that is set before me. I look unto Jesus, who is the Author and Perfecter of my faith.

Better is the end of a thing that the beginning thereof. The patient in spirit is better than the proud in spirit. I will ask the Lord to keep me from all anger and hastiness.

The Scriptures were written for my growth and learning, that I would through the patience and comfort they provide have hope. The God of patience and consolation is granting me the ability to be like-minded toward other believers through Jesus Christ (and to be patient toward them).

I receive God's promise, that those who wait upon the Lord will inherit the Earth. I glory in tribulations, knowing that tribulation works patience within me. This patience gives me experience, and this experience gives me hope. God's hope lifts me above all shame, because I know that His love is shed abroad in my heart by the Holy Ghost, which has been given to me.

I know this, that the trying of my heart works patience. I will let patience have her perfect work, that I may be perfect and entire, wanting nothing.

I thank God that He is establishing my heart, because I know the coming of the Lord draws near.

Related Scriptures: Galatians 5:22; Isaiah40:32; Psalm 27:14; Romans 8:25; Hebrews 6:12; Hebrews 10:35-37; Hebrews 12:1; Ecclesiastes 7:8-9; Romans 15:4-5; Psalm 40:1; Romans 5:3-5; James 1:3-4; James 5:7-8.

Personal Prayer: Heavenly Father, help me to be a patient believer who waits for the fulfillment of that which I know will eventually come. You have never failed me, and I believe every promise of your Word. In the patience you provide for me I will hold fast the profession of my faith without wavering, because I know you have been and always will be faithful to me. Thank you, Lord. I know that your integrity and your uprightness will preserve me as I wait upon you. In Jesus' name I pray, Amen.

A Promise to Claim: "The Lord takes pleasure in those who fear Him, in those who hope in His mercy" (Psalm 147:11, NKJV).

Words of Wisdom: *"Have patience with all things, but chiefly have patience with yourself. Do not lose courage in considering your imperfections, but instantly set about remedying them—every day begin the task anew"* (St. Francis de Sales).

Peace

Affirmation of Faith: Perfect peace is possible even in this world of sin.

> *Thou wilt keep him in perfect peace,*
> *whose mind is stayed on thee: because*
> *he trusteth thee.*

(ISAIAH 26:3)

Central Focus: Peace is a treasure which every believer may experience on a daily basis. It is possible because Jesus Christ himself is our peace. Peace, like patience, is a fruit of the indwelling Spirit. God helps us to develop the fruit of peace in all our relationships and responsibilities. Indeed, He is your peace!

Meditation on God's Promises to You: I trust in God and I will keep my mind stayed on Him. Therefore, I know He will keep me in His perfect peace.

Jesus is my peace. Hallelujah! Indeed, He is the Prince of peace, and I will follow Him. I am so thankful that the God of peace will be bruising Satan under my feet, and His grace shall ever be with me. The Lord is ordaining peace for me. He is the God of peace, and He will always be with me.

Being justified by faith, I have peace with God through the Lord Jesus Christ. I will let His peace rule in my heart, to which I have been called with my fellow-believers, and I am very thankful to Him for His peace.

I will both lie down in peace and sleep, for the Lord makes me to dwell in safety. The Lord is giving me His strength and He is blessing me with His peace.

Jesus has left His peace with me. He has given me His peace, but not as the world gives. Therefore, I will not let my heart be troubled, and I will not let it be afraid. I will be anxious about nothing, but in everything by prayer and supplication with thanksgiving I will let my requests be made known unto God.

As I do so, the peace of God, which surpasses all understanding will guard my heart and my mind through Christ Jesus. The great God of all hope is filling me with all joy and peace as I learn to trust Him. Because of this, I will overflow with hope in the power of the Holy Spirit.

The Lord Jesus has overcome the world. Though there is trouble in so many parts of the world, in Him I have great peace. I will ever be thankful to Him for His wonderful, supernatural peace.

Peace like a river is flowing through my soul.

Related Scriptures: Isaiah 26:3; Ephesians 2:14; Isaiah 9:6; Romans 16:20; Isaiah 26:12; Romans 5:1; Colossians 3:15; Psalm 4:8; Psalm 29:11; John 14:27; Philippians 4:6-7; Romans 15:13; John 15:33.

Personal Prayer: Heavenly Father, I know you love me and this realization brings deep and abiding peace to me. I will not let my heart be troubled about anything. I believe in you and in your Son, my Savior, the Lord Jesus Christ. I know that I will have a home with you in Heaven forever. I receive your promise of peace as I pray. Because your peace is my portion, I will never again be worried or afraid. In Jesus' name I pray, Amen.

A Promise to Claim: "My son, forget not my law; but let thine heart keep my commandments. For length of days, and long life, and peace, shall they add unto thee" (Proverbs 3:1-2).

Words of Wisdom: *"Rest is not a hallowed feeling that comes over us in church; it is the repose of a heart set deep in God"* (Henry Drummond).

39

Praise

Affirmation of Faith: Praise does so much for me. It is an emotional release that enables me to rise above life's circumstances and put my focus on God.

> *"Enter into his gates with thanksgiving, and into his courts with praise: be thankful unto him, and bless his name. For the Lord is good; his mercy is everlasting and his truth endureth to all generations"*

(PSALM 100:4-5)

Central Focus: Through praise we render unto God what is truly due to Him. He is our praiseworthy Father who has given us so many good things. Praise Him with all your heart. May your attitude be one of gratitude, and may you express your gratitude to God by praising Him all day long.

Meditation on God's Promises to You: I will praise the God of might and glory according to His righteousness. I will praise the Most High God with my whole heart and show forth all His marvelous works. I will be glad and rejoice in Him and sing praises to His name.

He is my strength and my shield, and my heart rests in Him. My heart greatly rejoices and I will praise Him with my singing. I will bless Him at all times, and His praise shall continually be in my mouth. My soul will make its boast in Him. The humble will hear thereof and be glad.

I will praise the Lord forever, because of all the things He's done for me and others. He is my God and I will seek Him early. His loving-kindness is better than life to me. Therefore, my lips shall praise Him, and thus I will bless Him while I live. I will lift up my hands in His name.

Praise waits for my God. I will bless His name forever. Every day I will bless Him. He is great and greatly to be praised. I will sing unto Him a new song every day.

God takes pleasure in His people, including me, and He beautifies the meek with His salvation. I will be joyful in the glory He's imparted to me. I will sing aloud upon my bed and let His high praises be in my mouth as I carry His two-edged sword in my hands.

I praise the Lord. I praise Him in the firmament of His power. I praise Him for His mighty acts. I praise Him according to His excellent greatness.

Praise the Lord!

Related Scriptures: Psalm 7; Psalm 9; Psalm 28; Psalm 34; Psalm 52; Psalm 63; Psalm 65; Psalm 111; Psalm 139; Psalm 145; Psalm 150.

Personal Prayer: Praise waits for you, O God. I will praise you with my whole heart. Thank you for taking pleasure in me and for beautifying the meek with your salvation. I will be joyful in the glory you've imparted to me. I will sing aloud upon my bed. I praise you, Lord, in the sanctuary. I praise you in the firmament of your power. I praise you for your mighty acts. I praise you according to your excellent greatness. In Jesus' name I pray (and praise), Amen.

A Promise to Claim: "And a voice came out of the throne, saying, Praise our God, all ye his servants, and ye that fear him both small and great" (Revelation 19:5).

Words of Wisdom: *"In the interior life of prayer [and praise] faithfulness points steadily to God and His purposes, away from self and its preoccupations"* (Evelyn Underhill).

40

Prayer

Affirmation of Faith: Prayer gives me direct-line access to my Father in Heaven. He awaits my prayer. True prayer is an ongoing dialogue with Him and I will engage in that dialogue with Him without ceasing.

> *"Hear me when I call, O God of my righteousness: thou hast enlarged me when I was in distress; have mercy upon me, and hear my prayer.*

(PSALM 4:1)

Central Focus: In the same way that air is vital to a person's physical well-being, prayer is vital to a person's spirit. Praying is time that is well spent, for it provides comfort, rest, security, and peace to every soul. Prayer should be the Christian's native air. It should be the atmosphere in which you live, and move, and have your being.

Meditation on God's Promises to You: God answers my prayers. I take delight in Him, and He gives me the desires of my heart. As I pray according to His will, He hears me and He grants my petitions. My heavenly Father knows what I need, and He meets my every need faithfully and lovingly. He supplies all my needs according to His riches in glory by Christ Jesus.

Whenever I ask Him, God gives His special answers to me. When I pray according to His plan and will, He always responds to my prayers and rewards my faith. When I knock, He opens the door. When I seek, He leads me to the answer. He is such a great and good God.

I will abide in Christ, and I will let His words abide in me. As a result, God will open the door to all He has for me, and I know He will give me whatever I ask of Him. Praise the Lord! My Father wants my joy to be full, and so He gives me the authority of Jesus' name, which fills me with joy and leads me to victory. Praying in His name always leads to victory and it brings answers to my prayers.

God gives every good and perfect gift to me. He lavishes His love upon me by inviting me into His banqueting hall. His banner over me is love. He has prepared a table for me, and He fills my cup to overflowing. I am so thankful that He always supplies my daily bread.

As I draw near to Him, He draws near to me. I will always pray in faith because I know from God's Word that He loves believing prayers, and He is committed to answering them. My Father is a rewarder of all who come to Him in faith. I believe in Him and in all the promises of His Word, and I look forward to all the rewards He has for me. When I pray, I express faith to Him, fully expecting His hand to move on my behalf.

God answers my prayers because He loves me. This leads me to trust in Him will all my heart, leaning not upon my own understanding. In all my ways I will acknowledge Him, and I know He will direct my paths.

Related Scriptures: Psalm 28:6; Psalm 37:4; 1 John 5:14; Matthew 6;8; Lamentations 3:23; Philippians 4:19; Hebrews 11:6; Matthew 7:8; John 15:7; John 16:23; James 1:17; Song of Solomon 2:4; Psalm 23:5; Luke 11:3; James 4:8; James 1:5-7; Hebrews 11:6; 1 John 2:23; Matthew 6:33; Psalm 136:12; Psalm 100:5; Proverbs 3:5-6.

Personal Prayer: Father, I want to give myself unto prayer. Thank you for hearing the voice of my supplications and receiving my prayer. I cast all my burdens upon you, Father, and, as I do so, I know you will sustain me because this is a prevailing promise from your Word. You are my sun and my shield, and I thank you for imparting your grace and glory to me. In Jesus' name I pray, Amen.

A Promise to Claim: "Now this is the confidence that we have in Him, that if we ask anything according to His will, He hears us" (1 John 5:14, NKJV).

Words of Wisdom: *"Prayer is the voice of faith"* (Horne).

41

Righteousness

Affirmation of Faith: Jesus is my righteousness. Without Him, I can do nothing, but through Him I can do all things. Hallelujah!

> *Hear me when I call, O God of my righteousness: thou hast enlarged me when I was in distress; have mercy upon me, and hear my prayer.*

(PSALM 4:1)

Central Focus: He who knew no sin became sin for us, that we might become His righteousness. (See 1 Corinthians 1:30.) As humans, we have no righteousness of our own. However, as believers, we have the righteousness of Christ which has been imparted to us. Receive His gift of righteousness and walk in it every day of your life.

Meditation on God's Promises to You: I am a servant of righteousness. God has freed me from all sin. With His help I am putting off the old man, which is corrupted through deceitful lusts. I am being renewed in the spirit of my mind, as I put on the new man, which is created in righteousness and true holiness.

I praise God for His promise that those who hunger and thirst after righteousness shall be filled. I do hunger and thirst after righteousness, and I am so thankful that God has made it possible for me to be filled with righteousness and its fruits.

With God's help, I will walk worthy unto Him with all pleasing, being fruitful in every good work, and increasing in the knowledge of Him. He is strengthening me with all might, according to His glorious power, unto all patience and longsuffering with joyfulness. I give thanks to the Father for making me meet to be a partaker of the inheritance of the saints in light. He has delivered me from the power of darkness and He has translated me into the Kingdom of His dear Son.

I receive tremendous comfort from the fact that I know His eyes are upon me and His ears are attentive to my cry. I hate evil, and I am so thankful that my Father-God guards my life and delivers me from the hand of the wicked. I am so thankful that He has shed His light upon me and given me deep and abiding joy.

I pray that my love will abound more and more in knowledge and in all judgement. God is filling me with the fruits of righteousness, which are by Christ Jesus unto His glory and praise. He is helping me to add goodness to my faith, knowledge to my goodness, self-control to my knowledge, perseverance to my self-control, godliness to my perseverance, brotherly kindness to my godliness, and love to my brotherly kindness.

Jesus has been made unto me wisdom, righteousness, sanctification, and redemption. The Lord is my Shepherd. Therefore, I shall not want. He makes me to lie down in green pastures, and He leads me beside the still waters. He restores my soul, and He leads me in the paths of righteousness for His name's sake. Surely goodness and mercy shall follow me all the days of my life, and I will dwell in His house forever.

Related Scriptures: Romans 6:18; Ephesians 4:23; Matthew 5:6; Colossians 1:10-13; Psalm 34:15; Psalm 97:10; Philippians 1:10-11; 2 Peter 1:5-8; 1 Corinthians 1:30; Psalm 23.

Personal Prayer: Dear Father in Heaven, thank you for the gift of righteousness you have given to me through your Son, Jesus Christ. He is my righteousness. You love righteousness, and so do I. Thank you for the realization that your countenance beholds me. Help me to walk uprightly, to work righteousness, and to speak truth in my heart. I know I shall behold your face in righteousness. In Jesus' name, Amen.

A Promise to Claim: "Being filled with the fruits of righteousness, which are by Jesus Christ, unto the glory and praise of God" (Philippians 1:11).

Words of Wisdom: *"The Son of God became a man to enable men to become sons of God"* (C. S. Lewis).

42

Salvation

Affirmation of Faith: My salvation is complete in Jesus Christ. He has made me whole.

Salvation belongeth unto the Lord; thy blessing is upon thy people.

(PSALM 3:8)

Central Focus: Jesus has saved us from sin, Satan, hell, and darkness. He has saved our soul and He has made us complete.

Meditation on God's Promises to You: Jesus is our Savior. We are not saved by our own works of righteousness, but according to His mercy, by the washing of regeneration and renewing of the Holy Ghost, which He shed on us abundantly through Jesus Christ. How I thank God that Jesus came to seek and to save that which was lost.

It is by His grace that we are saved. I confess the Lord Jesus with my mouth and I believe in my heart that God raised Him from the dead. Therefore, I know I am saved. I am in Christ; therefore, I am a new creation. Old things are passed away, and all things are become new.

Jesus promises that all who hear His Word and believe will have everlasting life. I know I shall not come into condemnation, because I have passed from death to life. It is by grace that I have been saved through faith, and that is not of myself. It is the gift of God, not of works, lest any man should boast. I am His workmanship, created in Christ Jesus unto good works, which God foreordained that I should walk in.

Because I have the Son, I have life. I am crucified with Christ, nevertheless I live. Yet, it is not I who lives, but Christ lives in me. The life which I now live in the flesh I live by faith in the Son of God, who loved me, and gave himself for me. I have been born again, not of corruptible seed, but of incorruptible, by the Word of God, which lives and abides forever.

In Christ I have redemption through His blood, the forgiveness of sins, according to the riches of His grace. Because I know the truth, as it is revealed in the Word of God, I am now free. Because Jesus has made me free, I know I am free indeed.

Having been made free from sin through the salvation that Jesus has provided for me, I am now a servant of God, who bears His fruit unto holiness. The end result is eternal life for me.

Related Scriptures: Titus 3:5-6; Luke 19:10; Ephesians 2:5; Romans 10:9; 2 Corinthians 5:17; John 5:24; Ephesians 2:8-10; 1 John 5:12; Galatians

2:20; 1 Peter 1:23; Ephesians 1:6-7; John 8:32, 36. Romans 6:22.

Personal Prayer: Heavenly Father, thank you for saving me through your Son, Jesus Christ, who is my Lord and Savior. I rejoice in the salvation you have provided for me. I will ever love you, O Lord my strength. You are my rock, my fortress, and my deliverer. You are my God and my strength. You are my salvation, and I will ever trust in you. Thank you for being my buckler and the horn of my salvation. My salvation comes solely from you. Thank you for all you have done, are doing, and will do for me. In the Savior's name I pray, Amen.

A Promise to Claim: "For the law of the Spirit of life in Christ Jesus hath made me free from the law of sin and death" (Romans 8:2).

Words of Wisdom: *"In Christ we are relaxed and at peace in the midst of the confusions, bewilderments, and perplexities of this life. The storm rages, but our hearts are at rest. We have found peace—at last!"* (Billy Graham).

Strength

Affirmation of Faith: Jesus is my strength. I can do all things through Him.

My soul melteth for heaviness; strengthen thou me according to your word.

(PSALM 119:28)

Central Focus: God's strength is available to us, even when we are weak. He is always our Almighty God.

Meditation on God's Promises to You: In returning and rest I shall be saved. In quietness and in confidence I find my strength. God is my rock, my deliverer, my strength, and the One in whom I trust. He is my buckler, the horn of my salvation, and my high tower. I will call upon Him. He is worthy to be praised.

God is our refuge and strength, a very present help in trouble. Therefore, I will not fear, though the earth be removed, and though the mountains be carried into the midst of the sea. Knowing God, I will be strong and of good courage. I will observe to do according to all His law. I will not turn to the left or the right, that I may prosper in everything I do and wherever I go. The Book of the Law (the Bible) will not depart out of my mouth. I will meditate in it day and night, and I will observe to do all that is written therein. Then my way will be prosperous and I will have good success. I take my stand upon His promises.

I will dwell in the secret place of the Most High and abide under the shadow of the Almighty. He truly is my safe place and my stronghold.

God lights my candle and He enlightens my darkness. By Him I can run through a troop and I have leaped over a wall. God's way is perfect. His Word is tried. He is a buckler to all those who trust in Him. He girds me with strength and makes my way perfect. He makes my feet like hinds' feet and sets me upon my high places. He teaches my hands to war, so that a bow of steel is broken by my arms. This is true strength.

The Lord is my strength and my shield. My heart trusts in Him and I am helped by Him. My heart greatly rejoices and with my song I will praise Him. The Lord is the God of my strength. He is the strength of my heart and my portion forever.

Who is strong like my Lord? The fear of the Lord is a fountain of life that enables me to depart from the snares of death. In the fear of the Lord I have strong confidence and a secure place of refuge. The Lord God will come with His strong hand and His strong arm. He will feed His flock like a shepherd. He will gather His lambs with His arm and carry them in His bosom.

The joy of the Lord is my strength.

Related Scriptures: Isaiah 30:15; Psalm 18:1-2; Psalm 46:1-2; Joshua 1:6-8; Psalm 46:1; Psalm 18:28-34; Psalm 28;7; Isaiah 40:10-11; Nehemiah 8:10.

Personal Prayer: Lord God, my strength, I give my life afresh to you, and I thank you that you always gird me with strength.

A Promise to Claim: "My grace is sufficient for you, for My strength is made perfect in weakness" (2 Corinthians 12:9-10, NKJV).

Words of Wisdom: *"When we cultivate the inner person through prayer, meditation on the Word, and submission to the Lord, then we can experience the joys of a disciplined and diligent life"* (Warren Wiersbe).

44

Temptation

Affirmation of Faith: I will seek God's help whenever temptation comes my way.

Blessed is the man that endureth temptation: for when he is tried, he shall receive the crown of life, which the Lord hath promised to them that love him.

(JAMES 1:12)

Central Focus: The choice is ours when temptations come. We can either resist them or yield to them. When we submit to God and resist the devil, he flees from us. (See James 4:7-9.) Temptation has no power over us when we stand upon God's promises that always prevail.

Meditation on God's Promises to You: The temptations I face are common to humanity. I know that God is faithful to me and He will not permit me to be tempted above what I am able to bear. He will make a way of escape for me.

The Lord knows how to deliver me out of all temptations. When I confess my sins, He is faithful and just to forgive me and to cleanse me from all unrighteousness. I will be sober and vigilant, because I know my adversary, the devil, as a roaring lion, walks about, seeking whom he may devour. I will resist him in faith.

Greater is He who is within me than he who is in the world. Hallelujah! As I submit my life to the Father and resist the devil, he flees from me. As I draw near to God, He draws near to me. Faith is the victory that overcomes the world, and I will let faith arise within me whenever temptations come. I will walk in faith every step of my way.

I am kept by the power of God though faith unto salvation, which is ready to be revealed in the last time. Therefore, I will greatly rejoice, because I know the trial of my faith is much more precious than of gold that perishes, though it be tried by fire. My faith will be found unto praise and honor and glory at the appearing of Jesus Christ, whom having not seen, I love. In Him, though I have never seen Him, I place all my faith and I rejoice with unspeakable joy that is full of glory.

Related Scriptures: 1 Corinthians 10:12-13; 2 Peter 2:9; 1 John 1:9; 1 Peter 5:8-9; 1 John 4:4; James 4:7-8; 1 John 5:4; 1 Peter 1:6-8.

Personal Prayer: Heavenly Father, you are so good to me. I thank you for your promise of overcoming power in the face of all temptations and difficulties.

When the enemy comes in like a flood, I know you will always be there to raise a standard against him. Thank you for your everlasting arms which are always there to support me. I know that you will enable me to always be victorious over all temptations. In Jesus' powerful name I pray, Amen.

A Promise to Claim: "No weapon formed against you shall prosper; and every tongue which rises against you in judgment you shall condemn. This is the heritage of the servants of the Lord. And their righteousness is from me" (Isaiah 54:17, NKJV).

Words of Wisdom: *"Faith is to believe what you do not see; the reward of this faith is to see what you believe"* (Augustine).

45

Thanksgiving

Affirmation of Faith: I will count my blessings and always praise God for all He has done and is doing in my life.

> *Rejoice evermore. Pray without ceasing. In everything give thanks: for this is the will of God in Christ Jesus concerning you.*

> (1 THESSALONIANS 5:16-18)

Central Focus: Living close to God always engenders thankfulness. This happens because, as we do so, we experience His goodness in every part of our lives. Draw close to Him, and He will draw close to you.

Meditation on God's Promises to You: It is wonderful to be able to serve the Lord with gladness and to come before His presence with singing. He is my Creator, and I am a sheep in His pasture. I will enter His gates with thanksgiving and go into His courts with praise. I will be thankful unto Him and bless His holy name, for He is good. His mercy is everlasting, and His truth endures to all generations.

I will let the peace of God rule in my heart, and I will be thankful at all times. I will let the Word of Christ dwell in me richly in all wisdom, as I teach and admonish others with Psalms and spiritual songs. I will sing with grace in my heart unto the Lord. Whatever I do in word or deed, I will do all in the name of the Lord Jesus, giving thanks to God, the Father.

I will praise the name of God with a song, and I will magnify Him with thanksgiving. I will make a joyful noise unto the rock of my salvation. I will go before His presence with thanksgiving and make a joyful noise unto Him with Psalms, for the Lord is a great God, and a great King above all gods.

I will rejoice in the Lord always, and I will be anxious for nothing. In everything, by prayer and supplication with thanksgiving, I will let my requests be made known unto God. As I do so, I know His wonderful peace that surpasses all understanding will guard my heart and my mind through Christ Jesus.

It is such a good thing to give thanks unto the Lord and to sing praises unto Him. I will show forth His loving-kindness in the morning and His faithfulness every night. He has made me glad through His work, and I will triumph in the work of His hands.

O death, where is your sting? O grave, where is your victory? The sting of death is sin, but thanks be to God who gives me the victory through my Lord Jesus Christ.

Related Scriptures: Psalm 100; Colossians 3:15-17; Psalm 69:30; Psalm 95:1-3; Philippians 4:4-7; Psalm 92:1-4; 1 Corinthians 15:55-57.

Personal Prayer: Father God, I want to thank you and praise you, for you have been so good to me. I love you with all my heart. Thank you for delivering my soul from death, my eyes from tears, and my feet from falling. I will walk before you in the land of the living. It is good and pleasant to sing praises to you and to be thankful. Therefore, I sing unto you with thanksgiving, and I praise your holy name. Thank you for strengthening the bars of my gates and giving me your glorious peace. In Jesus' name I pray, Amen.

A Promise to Claim: "A merry heart doeth good like a medicine: but a broken spirit drieth the bones" (Proverbs 17;22).

Words of Wisdom: *"Faith sees God, and God sees faith. Faith sees God, who is invisible, and God sees even that little faith, which would be invisible to others"* (Charles Spurgeon).

46

Trust

Affirmation of Faith: Through God's grace I will trust in the Lord at all times.

> *He shall not be afraid of evil tidings: his heart is fixed, trusting in the Lord.*

(PSALM 112:7)

Central Focus: Trusting involves a deep level of faith that cannot be disturbed, no matter what the circumstances may be.

Meditation on God's Promises to You: Through God I shall do valiantly, for I know that it is He who will tread down my enemies. As I learn to trust Him implicitly, I will cast all my cares upon Him, for I know He truly cares for me.

I know that all things work together for good in my life, because I love and trust God and I've been called according to His purposes. I am greatly blessed by Him, as I trust Him and place all my hope in Him. As a result, the Bible promises that I will be like a tree planted by the waters, a tree that spreads out its roots by the river, a tree that will not be affected by the heat, and a tree with leaves that are always green. I will be fruitful even in a time of drought.

I will say of the Lord that He is my refuge and my fortress. He is my God, and I will ever trust in Him. He will surely deliver me from the snare of the fowler and from the noisome pestilence. He will cover me with His feathers, and under His wings I will trust. His truth shall be my shield and buckler.

The Lord always helps me and delivers me. He has delivered me from the wicked, because I trust in Him. Therefore, I will not fear, though the Earth be removed and though the mountains be carried into the midst of the sea.

When I am afraid, I will trust in the Lord. In God I will praise His Word. In God I have placed my trust. I will not fear what flesh can do to me. He has delivered my soul from death and my feet from falling, that I may walk before Him in the light of the living.

Every word of God is pure; He is a shield to them that put their trust in Him. The Lord is a shield for me. He is my glory and the lifter of my head. I cried unto the Lord with my voice, and He heard me out of His holy hill. I laid down and slept, and I awakened, for the Lord sustained me. I will not be afraid of ten thousands of people that have set themselves against me round about.

He is keeping me in the path He has set out for me, so that my footsteps slip not. I have called upon Him, for I know He hears me. He inclines His ear unto me and He hears my speech. He is showing me His marvelous loving-kindness. He has saved me by His right hand, as I have learned to put my trust in Him. It thrills me to know that He will keep me as the apple of His eye and hide me under the shadow of His wings.

Related Scriptures: Psalm 60:12; 1 Peter 5:7; Romans 8:28; Jeremiah 17:7-8; Psalm 91:2-4; Psalm 37:40; Psalm 46:2; Psalm 56:3-4, 13; Proverb 30:5; Psalm 3:3-6; Psalm 17:5-8.

Personal Prayer: In you, O Lord, do I put my trust. Let me never be put to confusion. Be my strong habitation, Father, whereunto I shall continually resort. You are my hope, and I place all my trust in you. Through your grace, I will trust in you with all my heart without leaning upon my own understanding. In all my ways I will acknowledge you, and I know you will direct my steps. Thank you for being my trustworthy Father and for blessing me with so many good things. In Jesus' name I pray, Amen.

A Promise to Claim: "He that handleth a matter wisely shall find good: and whoso trusteth in the Lord, happy is he" (Proverbs 16:30).

Words of Wisdom: *"Faith does not eliminate questions. But faith knows where to take them"* (Elisabeth Elliot).

47

Wisdom

Affirmation of Faith: I do not have to ask God for wisdom, because He has already given it to me. I will walk in His wisdom each step of my way.

Happy is the man that findeth wisdom, and the man that getteth understanding.

(PROVERBS 3:13)

Central Focus: Wisdom is the principal thing. Therefore, hold on to the wisdom God has given to you. (See Proverbs 4:7.) The fear of the Lord is the beginning of wisdom for your life.

Meditation on God's Promises to You: This is wisdom: to retain God's words, keep His commandments, and live. I will get wisdom and understanding, and I will not forget it. I will not forsake wisdom, because I know it will preserve me and keep me. Wisdom truly is the principal thing. Therefore, I will cling to it and every form of spiritual understanding.

God is the source of all true wisdom, and He gives me His wisdom in all the decisions of my life. His wisdom is always with me. My lips will spread both wisdom and knowledge to others, and I will cherish spiritual understanding.

I know that wisdom is better than weapons of war, gold, silver, rubies, and strength. The wisdom of God has been imparted to me and it blesses me and makes me happy. Nothing I desire compares with wisdom. Long life, riches, honor, and peace are supplied to me through God's wisdom. Its ways are pleasant and its pathways lead to peace.

Wisdom is a tree of life to me. I am so thankful for the secret wisdom of God that has been hidden through the ages and given to me through His Word. He destined this wisdom for me to have before time began. I will show forth His wisdom by a good life and deeds done in humility. Through God's grace I will let the Word of Christ dwell in me richly, as I teach and admonish others with all wisdom.

God's wisdom is pure, peace-loving, considerate, submissive, full of mercy and good fruit. It is also impartial and sincere. With His help I will walk in wisdom forevermore. I will ask God for an undivided heart, that I may fear, honor, and respect Him always.

I praise God for the full riches of understanding that He has given to me. It enables me to know His mystery and to know Christ more fully. In Him are hidden all the treasures of wisdom and knowledge for which I am very thankful indeed.

God is filling me with the knowledge of His will through spiritual wisdom and understanding. I want to live a life that is worthy of Him. I want to please Him in every way and bear fruit in every good work, as I grow in my knowledge of Him.

I will never forget that a house is built by wisdom and it is established by understanding. Through knowledge its rooms are filled with rare and beautiful treasures. God's wisdom gives me strength and power.

Eye has not seen and ear has not heard, neither has it entered into the human heart all the things that God has prepared for those who love Him. These things have been revealed to me by His Spirit who searches all things, including the deep, spiritual things. I choose not to speak with human wisdom, but only with the wisdom of the Holy Spirit.

Related Scriptures: Proverbs 4:5-7; James 1:3-6; Ecclesiastes 9:13-18; 1 Corinthians 2:7-8; James 3:13; Colossians 3:16; James 3:17; Psalm 86:11; Colossians 2:1; Colossians 1:9-10; Proverbs 24:3-5; 1 Corinthians 2:9-14.

Personal Prayer: Father, I know you desire truth in my inner parts, and so I ask you to help me know wisdom deep within. Teach me to number my days, Lord God, so that I would apply my heart to wisdom. Realizing that wisdom stems from fearing and respecting you, I give my life to you afresh and I honor you as the almighty God of wisdom. Father, I will walk in wisdom and follow your leading each step of my way. In the wise and wonderful name of Jesus I pray, Amen.

A Promise to Claim: "When wisdom entereth into thine heart, and knowledge is pleasant unto thy soul; discretion shall preserve thee, understanding shall keep thee" (Proverbs 2:10-11).

Words of Wisdom: *"Never mistake knowledge for wisdom. One helps you make a living; the other helps you make a life"* (Sandra Carey).

48

Witnessing

Affirmation of Faith: The Holy Spirit gives me the power to be an effective witness. I will let His power flow through me to others.

> *But ye shall receive power, after that the*
> *   Holy ghost is come upon you:*
> *and ye shall be witnesses unto me.*

(ACTS 1:8)

Central Focus: People need to know that God loves them and that Jesus died for them. Let them know this, and lead them to a saving knowledge of the Lord Jesus Christ. Do not be ashamed of the Gospel of Jesus Christ, for it is the power of God unto salvation to all who believe.

Meditation on God's Promises to You: The Spirit of the Lord is upon me. He empowers me to be a witness for my Lord and Savior, Jesus Christ, wherever I go—at home, at work, in the neighborhood, in the marketplace, and even in the church. Through His power I will become an effective witness for Jesus Christ.

A person who wins souls is wise. I want to be such a wise person. Therefore, I commit myself to being a vibrant witness at all times. I know the Lord will lead me to the ones who need Him, and He will always give me the right words to say.

I have received a commission from the Lord Jesus. As His disciple, I will go into all the world and share the gospel with others. The power of the Holy Spirit fills me, and I will never be ashamed of the Gospel of Jesus Christ because I know it is the power of God unto salvation for all who will believe.

Therefore, I will go out into the highways and byways of this busy world in an effort to find those who need the Savior. He will guide me each step of the way as I do so. His perfect love casts out all fear from me as I witness for Him. My goal is to reach the lost, rescue the perishing, and care for the dying.

I thank God that I am the salt of the Earth, and I want my life to always make others thirsty for Jesus. I am also the light of the world, and I want my life to reflect God's light to others. I will be a witness for Jesus Christ throughout this day, as I receive and share His enabling power. I will be His ambassador and representative wherever I go.

Related Scriptures: Luke 4:18; Acts 1:8; 2 Corinthians 5:20; Proverbs 11:30; Isaiah 43:12; Psalm 5:8; Mark 13:11; Matthew 28:29-20; Romans 1:16; Luke 14:23; Psalm 48:14; 1 John 4:18; Matthew 5:13; Matthew 5:14; Ephesians 6:20.

Personal Prayer: Father, thank you for allowing me to be your ambassador wherever I go. With your help, I will be your faithful witness at all times. May the words of my mouth and the meditations of my heart always be acceptable in your sight, O my Lord and Redeemer. Fill me with your Spirit, Father. Through Him I will be a witness to others. Help me to develop a sensitivity to others that will permit me to hear the cries of their hearts in the same way you do, Father. Let your powerful love flow through me and reach out to others. In Jesus' mighty name I pray, Amen.

A Promise to Claim: "And for me, that utterance may be given unto me, that I may open my mouth boldly, to make known the mystery of the gospel, for which I am an ambassador in bonds: that therein I may speak boldly, as I ought to speak" (Ephesians 6:19-20).

Words of Wisdom: *"Only one life will soon be past; only what's done for Christ will last"* (C.T. Studd).

Word of God

Affirmation of Faith: God's Word will guide me each step of my way. I love the Word of God and I will live according to its precepts.

> *For the word of God is quick, and powerful, and sharper than*
> *any twoedged sword, piercing even to the dividing asunder of*
> *soul and spirit, and of the joints and marrow, and is a discerner*
> *of the thoughts and intents of the heart.*

(HEBREWS 4:12)

Central Focus: Gods' Word is truth. Be sure to walk in the light of truth it sheds each step of your way.

Meditation on God's Promises to You: God's Word is a lamp unto my feet and a light unto my path. It is living and powerful, and it imparts faith to my heart. I will study it diligently so I can be a worker who is never ashamed, because I will know how to rightly divide His Word. All Scripture is given by inspiration, and it provides me with doctrine, reproof, correction, and instruction in righteousness so that I will be able to do good works for my Lord.

I realize that I do not live by bread alone, but by every word that proceeds from the mouth of God. His Word declares that I have power over the enemy. His Word is truth, and it sanctifies me. The Word of God renews my mind. It is the sword of the Spirit. God's Word keeps me from sin. I will hide His Word in my heart so that I will not sin against Him.

I thank God that His Word has the power to heal me and deliver me from all negative influences in my life. This truth inspires me to praise the Lord for His goodness and for His wonderful works in my life. God's testimonies are wonderful, and my soul will treasure them and keep them. When His Word enters my spirit, it fills me with light and gives me understanding. Hs Word also brings cleansing to my soul.

When I was born again it was by the incorruptible seed of the Word of God, which lives and abides forever. His Word endures forever. In the beginning was the Word, and the Word was with God, and the Word was God. Yes, Jesus is the living Word of God. All things were made by Him, and without Him was not anything made that was made. In Him was life, and His life was the light of men.

Yes, there is great and eternal power in the Word of God.

Related Scriptures: Psalm 119:105; Hebrews 4:12; Romans 10:17; 2 Timothy 2:15; 2 Timothy 3:16-17; Matthew 4:4; Luke 4; John 17:17; Ephesians 5:26; Ephesians 6:17; Psalm 119:11; Psalm 107:20-21; Psalm 119:129; Psalm 119:130; John 15:3; 1 Peter 1:23; 1 Peter 1:25; John 1:1-4; 2 Peter 3:5.

Personal Prayer: Teach me, O Lord, your ways through your Word. Help me to claim your promises every day. I will keep your statutes to the end. Give me understanding and I will keep your law. Through your grace I will observe your Word with all my heart. Lead me in the paths of your commandments, for in your Word I find my delight. Incline my heart to your Word. I love your Word, and it is my fervent desire to follow its direction throughout my life. In Jesus' name I pray, Amen.

A Promise to Claim: "Forever, O Lord, thy word is settled in heaven. Thy faithfulness is unto all generations: thou hast established the earth, and it abideth. . . .O how I love thy law! It is my meditation all the day" (Psalm 1119:89-97).

Words of Wisdom: *"I, as a human, do not become the power or love or wisdom of God; I merely contain Him who is all of these, and everything"* (Norman Grubb).

Worship

Affirmation of Faith: Worship allows me to go directly to the Father with adoration, praise, and wonder. This I will do every day of my life.

O come, let us worship and bow down: let us kneel before the Lord our maker.

(PSALM 95:6)

Central Focus: Worship in spirit and in truth enables you to know God as He really is. We worship Him for who He is, and we praise Him for all He is doing and has done. In His presence there is fullness of joy. Experience His presence through worship.

Meditation on God's Promises to You: As I worship the Lord, I ascribe glory to His name. I come before Him and worship Him in the spirit of holiness. I exalt Him as I worship at His footstool, for I know He is holy. I shout for joy to Him and I worship Him with gladness. I come before Him with joyful songs.

It is my desire to worship the Lord in spirit and in truth, for I know He wants that from me. He is my strength and my song. He has become my salvation. He is my God and I will praise and worship Him. I will exalt His name forevermore.

The main thing I seek is to dwell in the Lord's house all the days of my life, as I gaze upon His beauty and worship in His holy temple. Better is one day in the Lord's house than a thousand elsewhere. I would rather be a doorkeeper in the Lord's house than to dwell anywhere else.

How lovely is your dwelling place, O Lord, the Almighty! My soul yearns, even faints, for God's courts. My heart and my soul cry out to Him. I lift up holy hands to Him. I shout for joy to Him, and I worship Him with gladness in my heart and soul. I come before His presence in worship. He is my God and Creator. I am but a sheep in His pasture.

I enter into His gates with thanksgiving and I go into His courts with praise. I am thankful unto Him, and I bless His holy name. He is good and His mercy is everlasting. His truth endures to all generations. Praise His holy name!

I bless the Lord, for He is great. He is clothed with honor and majesty. I give thanks to Him, as I call upon His name and make His deeds known to others. I sing unto Him and I talk of all His wondrous works. I glory in His holy name and I rejoice as I seek and worship Him.

As I worship the Lord, I remember all His marvelous works, wonders, and the judgements of His mouth. I love the Lord, because I know He has heard my voice and my supplications. I thank Him for inclining His ear unto me. I will call upon Him as long as I live.

I am so happy to be the servant of the Lord, the son of His handmaiden. I thank Him for loosening my bonds. I offer unto Him the sacrifice of thanksgiving, and I call upon His name. I will pay my vows unto Him and worship Him in the presence of His people.

My worship belongs to God alone.

Related Scriptures: 1 Chronicles 16:29; Psalm 99:5; Psalm 100:1; John 4:23-24; Exodus 15:2; Psalm 27:4 Psalm 84:1-2; 1 Timothy 2:8; Psalm 00:1; Psalm 100:2-5; Psalm 194:1; Psalm 105:1-5: Psalm 116:1-2; Psalm 116:16-19.

Personal Prayer: O Lord my God, I draw near to you in worship, and, as I do so, I know you are drawing near to me. I come into your presence in the multitude of your mercies, as I honor and worship you. Lead me, Father, in your righteousness and make your way straight before my face. You alone are God. Teach me your ways as I worship you. I want to walk in your truth. I love you with all my heart. In Jesus' name, Amen.

A Promise to Claim: "Exalt ye the Lord our God, and worship at His footstool; for he is holy" (Psalm 99:5).

Words of Wisdom: *"A man can no more diminish God's glory by refusing to worship Him than a lunatic can put out the sun by scribbling the word 'darkness' on the walls of his cell"* (C. S. Lewis).

PART VII

Afterword

As you have meditated on God's *Promises That Prevail*, I'm sure your faith has been strengthened, your mind has been renewed, and you've drawn closer to God. May you always prevail in prayer and believe all God's promises.

The Bible says, "The effectual fervent prayer of a righteous man availeth much" (James 5:16). Lift up the promises of God as you pray and see what God will do for you, but always be sure to pray in faith, for faith is the victory that overcomes the world.

Keep on keeping on. Essentially, this is what prevailing means. Never give up. God is always with you. He knows what you have need of even before you express it to Him. He wants to hear your faith-filled prayers, and He wants to bless you.

Never forget that He is watching over His Word, and He always will. "Then the Lord said to me, Thou hast well seen: for I will hasten my word to perform it" (Jeremiah 1:12). Let God perform His Word in your life.

The words of this hymn provide a fitting conclusion for this book: "Great is thy faithfulness! Great is thy faithfulness! Morning by morning new mercies I see; all I have needed thy hand has provided; great is thy faithfulness, Lord, unto me!" (Thomas O. Chisholm).

PURE GOLD CLASSICS

TIMELESS TRUTH IN A DISTINCTIVE, BEST-SELLING COLLECTION

An Expanding Collection of the Best-Loved Christian Classics of All Time.

AVAILABLE AT FINE BOOKSTORES.

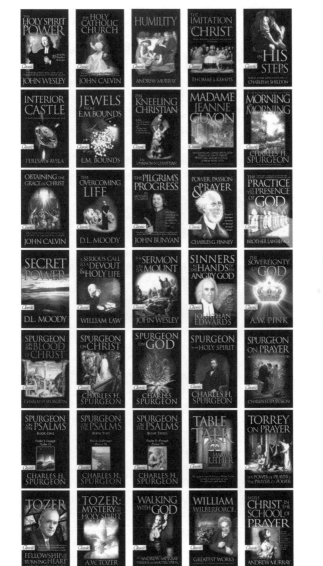

Prayers That Change Things

by Lloyd Hildebrand

More than 160,000 copies have been sold in the series. These mass-market paperbacks contain prayers that are build from the promises of God and teaching that is thoroughly scriptural.

978-1-61036-105-7
MMP / 192 pages

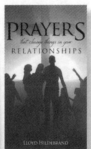

978-0-88270-012-0
MMP / 232 pages

978-0-88270-743-3
MMP / 232 pages

978-1-61036-126-2
MMP / 216 pages

978-1-61036-132-3
MMP / 248 pages

978-1-61036-141-5
MMP / 256 pages

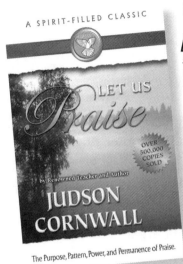

A SPIRIT-FILLED CLASSIC

LET US Praise

OVER 500,000 COPIES SOLD

by Renowned Teacher and Author

JUDSON CORNWALL

The Purpose, Pattern, Power, and Permanence of Praise.

Let Us Praise
by Judson Cornwall

Let Us Praise has sold more than 500,000 copies through the years since Judson Cornwall wrote it. Its teaching about praise continues to minister to thousands of believers around the world who are learning about the power of praise in their lives. Judson writes, "May the ministry of praise that this book teaches find an expression in the Body of Christ far beyond the areas covered in *Let Us Praise*."

This dynamic book covers many important topics:

- *The importance of praise*
- *Why praise is vital in a believer's life*
- *How we should praise the Lord*
- *What does the Bible teach about praise?*
- *The purpose of praise*

These are only some of the topics that Cornwall covers in this Spirit-filled Classic. He answers the readers' questions about praise—its purpose, its patterns, its power, and its permanence.

The power of praise is a power that changes circumstances, personal perspectives, and the human heart. Yes, "It is a good thing to give thanks unto the Lord, and to sing praises unto thy name, O Most High" (Psalm 92:1).

ISBN: 978-0-88270-992-5
TPB / 168 pages

"The Consummate Apologetics Bible...

Everything you ever need to share your faith."

"The Evidence Bible is the reservoir overflowing with everything evangelistic—powerful quotes from famous people, amazing anecdotes, sobering last words, informative charts, and a wealth of irrefutable evidence to equip, encourage, and enlighten you, like nothing else. I couldn't recommend it more highly."

– Kirk Cameron

"Honestly, this is my very FAVORITE Bible of all..."

"I have purchased roughly 30 copies of this Bible to give as gifts."

"Wow! What an awesome Bible!"

"Amazing. Just amazing."

"Love, love, love this Bible... I can't recommend it enough."

"A fantastic study Bible! Very grateful to have it!"

Compiled by Ray Comfort

This edition of The Evidence Bible includes notes, commentaries, and quotations that make it a comprehensive work of apologetics and evangelism that will be helpful to every believer. It covers a variety of practical topics, including the following:

- How to answer objections to Christianity
- How to talk about Christ with people of other religions
- How to counter evolutionary theories, while providing evidence for God's creation
- How to grow in Christ
- How to use the Ten Commandments when witnessing

There is no other Bible like this one. Every soul-winner who wants to lead others to Christ will want a copy of The Evidence Bible, because it provides springboards for preaching and witnessing, shares insights from well-known Christian leaders, gives points for open-air preaching, reveals the scientific facts contained within the Bible, and supplies the believer with helpful keys to sharing one's faith. The Bible is "the sword of the Spirit," and this edition of the Bible will motivate believers to become true spiritual warriors in their daily interactions with others.

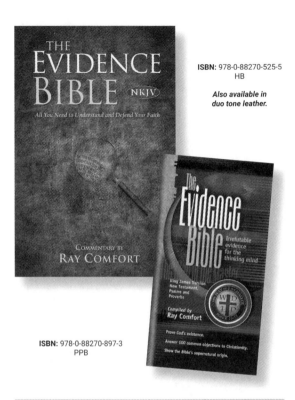

ISBN: 978-0-88270-525-5
HB

*Also available in
duo tone leather.*

ISBN: 978-0-88270-897-3
PPB

Also from Ray Comfort:

World Religions in a Nutshell

Ray Comfort

This book compares and contrasts
Christianity with various religions .
. . and includes sample witnessing
conversations and testimonies of
people from various faiths who
have turned to Christ.

ISBN: 978-88270-901-7
TPB

More from Rev. Dr. Phil Goldfedder

D R. PHILLIP GOLDFEDDER graduated from Albright College and New York Medical College. Following a neurosurgical residency, he practiced as a neurosurgeon for thirty-seven years. He became disappointed with the limited number of patients healed with chronic or terminal disease. He had a mid-life crisis when Jesus healed him of chronic, intractable pain. God called him into the healing ministry where he saw more people healed by the laying on of hands than he did with a scalpel. Dr. Goldfedder is an ordained minister, holds an honorary doctorate in Christian Education.

978-1-61036-117-0
TPB / 192 pages

978-0-88270-704-4
TPB / 138 pages

978-1-61036-101-9
TPB / 512 pages

978-1-61036-090-6
TPB / 174 pages

978-0-9824145-7-6
TPB / 175 pages

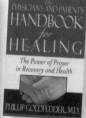

978-0-98241-456-95
TPB / 176 pages